DEMONS OF THE
HELLMOUTH
A GUIDE FOR SLAYERS

NANCY HOLDER

Foreword by Anthony Stewart Head

TITAN BOOKS

Foreword by
ANTHONY STEWART HEAD

Back in 1995–1996, I was in LA for pilot season. I had just turned down a TV show about the occult, which had a guaranteed order of about 64 episodes; it just didn't appeal to me. My agent thought I was insane. About a week later, I was sent a script for something called *Buffy the Vampire Slayer*. I'd heard of the movie, but I'd never seen it and thought how typically Hollywood it was to be making a TV show of it. That night, I sat in a Tex-Mex restaurant on Fourth Street in Santa Monica, turning the pages excitedly and literally laughing out loud at some of the funnier moments (people around me actually turned to look at the lonely Englishman falling about at his table)—it was a great script. On my way over to the Valley to meet Marcia Shulman (casting) and Joss Whedon, I stopped in at a friend's house in Toluca Lake for a coffee. I told him that I really, really wanted this job, unlike anything else I had read all season, and he said, "Then you'll get it."

There's something extraordinarily engaging about Joss. Both he and Marcia were lovely, and very un-LA—I think the meeting may even have been in the front room of Marcia's house. Anyway, the way I saw Giles, he could either be softly spoken and slightly reticent like Prince Charles (I do a passable impression of him,) or very dry like Alan Rickman's Sheriff of Nottingham. I asked Joss which he'd like and he helpfully said . . . "Both, please." Whatever I did—I have no idea what I did—it seemed to go down well.

And so, Giles was born. The process that followed is well-documented, apart from adding that the night before my test for the studio, my agent suggested I watch the Buffy movie to get up to speed. As I went into the Fox offices Joss was standing by the door, greeting us all, and I smugly told him that I'd now seen the film—I've rarely seen a look of such pure horror on a man's face, unless of course they're confronted with a vampire. Needless to say, the series was not the movie.

Filming Buffy gave me some of the best experiences of my career. The writing was consistently wonderful, the story arcs constantly challenging and the characters always growing and developing as people. Joss's writing called for our characters to be affected by the life-changing events going on around them—something that didn't often happen in episodic television at the time. So many attributes of Buffy have been adopted by other shows since we first aired in 1997. The vampire hero is an obvious one, but the style, the humor, and the storytelling have become a part of the culture.

Reading this book has reminded me of the enormous fun we had, exploring this weird and wonderful world of Joss's. So many demons, so many rituals, so many unpronounceable names—I often had to write them on Post-it notes and stick them out of sight of the camera. Most of all, the characters themselves: wonderfully rounded, their backstories brimming with detail, which allowed us, as actors, to invest completely in this world. The little notes in this book's margins (from Buffy, Willow et al.,) bring back the wonderful friendships that Joss and the writers created for us; it was a glorious playground, constantly changing and developing.

I hope you enjoy reading this as much as I have—it has brought back many happy memories for me.

Including helpful translations into actual English from Yours Truly so you won't flunk the written.
—B

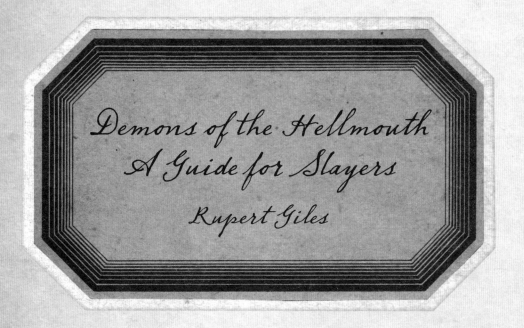

Demons of the Hellmouth
A Guide for Slayers

Rupert Giles

PLUS LOTS OF COOL MAGICS AND, YOU KNOW, WITCHY STUFF.
☺ —W

Me, I think it'd be more fun for you guys to be surprised, but can't lie that this will steer you around the curves.
— Faith

Nice, job, G-man!
—X

The earth is doomed.
—G

Contents

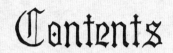

My Field Guide to Demons of the Hellmouth
1

Part I: Vampires
06

Part II: Demons
44

Part III: Other Forces of Darkness
110

Conclusion
146

Apocalypses & Magic Spells
148

My Final Thoughts
151

My Field Guide to Demons of the Hellmouth

This is my attempt to preserve for posterity what I've learned about the Demons of the Sunnydale Hellmouth and the Slayers who have so valiantly battled them. I have been collecting these notes for some time, and I preserved my findings in the Magic Box until it was destroyed. As you can see, busy hands have been aware of these pages for some time. There are notes scribbled in the margins by Buffy, Faith, Willow, and it would appear, Xander.

I'M SORRY, GILES. —W ☹

Hey, I resent that remark! I'm an integral part of the group! —X

I wrote some of the entries immediately after an encounter with a race of demons or a "Big Bad," as we have come to call our most dangerous and powerful foes. Others I wrote later, or I added information to old entries as I gathered it. It is my hope that Slayers everywhere will benefit from my attempt to catalog the demons, monsters, and other forces of darkness that may confront us again as we continue to combat evil.

After a little therapeutic shopping! —B

The Slayers

It is perhaps ironic that the Slayer Line itself is demonic in origin: long, long ago, the Shadow Men chained The First Slayer, Sineya, also called the Primitive, to a rock and forced her to ingest a demon. This infused her with the superpowers we have come to associate with the Slayer—speed, strength, healing—as well as prophetic dreaming. When Buffy returned to the dimension of the Shadow Men for help against The First Evil, she saw this demon, and described it to me as "living black smoke." It sought to merge with her, and she refused it entry.

And punning! —B

WHICH IS HARDER THAN IT SOUNDS! —W

The First Slayer saw herself as a dealer in death and little else, and from her lonely, stark existence, various traditions sprang up around the Slayer, including the words that describe the Slayer's calling: *I had a dream about two Slayers merging once... —X*

In every generation there is a chosen one. *She alone* will stand against the vampires, the demons, and the forces of darkness. She is the Slayer.

Except for now. Thanks, Will. —B ☺ *—W*

The Watchers

As you know, the Shadow Men became the Watchers, and they formed the Watchers Council of Britain. It comprised men and women, although the Slayers were always girls—quite young. Buffy was called to be a Slayer when she was fifteen. She faced death for the first time at sixteen, at which time a new Slayer was called. But perhaps I'm getting a bit ahead of my story.

While we're young, Giles . . .
—B

Like generations of Watchers before me, I instructed my Slayer in time-honored battle techniques—martial arts and ancient weapons such as quarterstaffs, swords, crossbows, and simple wood stakes. Demons and vampires are older even than the Slayer Line itself, and thus quite skilled in the ancient ways of battle. Rarely has an attempt to use modern weaponry worked out well, even for that most modern of Slayers, Buffy—save, perhaps, for when we destroyed the Judge with a rocket launcher, and deployed a robot to distract Glorificus the Hellgod.

Good for fighting Friar Tuck
—B

Hello, flying fatality!
—B

Running away? Also a time-honored battle technique.
—X

RIP, Buffybot!
—B

Watcher's Codex
D.R.L.F
A Rare & Curious Manuscript

*This tome has proven very useful through the years.
Even Buffy has consulted it. On her own. —G*

Last time I did that, I dreamed
about my mom. —D

JUST BEFORE WE FIGURED
OUT WHAT THE FIRST WAS.
—W

And not the First Bank of
Delaware, either. —X

The Guardians

The Slayer's last and most primal weapon was the Scythe, forged in secret by the Guardians†—mystical women who had set themselves the task of watching the Watchers. The Scythe was designed to be wielded by the Slayer to destroy the last pure demon on the Hellmouth. The last Guardian gave it to Buffy ... and yet, at that time, there were two Slayers in existence: Buffy and Faith. I believe the Guardian determined Buffy's primacy in the Slayer line because although she did die when she was sixteen, she was brought back, and so she is the "root" of the current Slayer family tree. (Please see my further discussion of the Slayer Line Disruption.) Be that as it may, Buffy shared the Scythe with all the new Slayers at the Final Battle, to quite good effect.

"Quite good effect?" Giles, we WON! —B&F

Buzz the scythe gives off feels freaky! —F

You never met a footnote you didn't love. —B

---

†**CONTINUATION OF WATCHERS DISCUSSION**

We Watchers never knew of the existence of the Guardians. And a good thing too, I must say, as the Council did not acquit itself terribly well in aiding Buffy through the years. Quentin Travers forced me to weaken Buffy with drugs in secret so that she could undergo the Cruciamentum, *a barbaric exercise in cruelty designed to weed out inferior Slayers on their eighteenth birthdays. With only her wits to keep her alive, a Slayer who does not pass the test is replaced when she dies.*

So over! —B

    I called off this test and so was replaced myself, with Wesley Wyndam-Pryce, who was officious and arrogant and did more harm than good.

You got that right, yo! —F

    Before he arrived, however, Mrs. Gwendolyn Post, an ex-Watcher fired for her use of the Dark Arts, presented herself as Faith's new Watcher. Post sought only to use Faith, and died as a result of her own treachery.

AND I AM GLAD! —F

Slayer Line Disruption

Because Buffy perished at the hands of the Master at the age of sixteen (<u>and was brought back through CPR</u>), a new Slayer was called. This was Kendra Young, whose Watcher was Sam Zabuto. Thus we had two Slayers, an unprecedented situation in the annals of the Watchers Council. As it turned out, this duplication was quite a lucky thing, as it led Buffy to her conclusion of sharing her power with all the potential Slayers.

Thanks, Xand! —B

Buffy the Vampire Slayer

At the onset of our relationship together, I was determined to mold Buffy into the image of a Slayer I had been trained to expect: dutiful, unquestioning, friendless, secretive. <u>Like Kendra, in fact</u>. Instead, Buffy broke that mold and became her own Slayer. Most importantly, she had *friends*.

I knew she was your favorite! —B

She and I have both suffered terrible losses: Spike, Jenny. Boys whose lives she could not risk, such as Scott Hope and Owen Thurman; women who were fearful of my world, like Olivia. But we have had excellent companions along the way: Willow, Xander, Cordelia (in her way), and for a time, Tara, Anya, Oz (Daniel Osbourne), and Riley. <u>And, of course, Angel.</u> *Of course! —B*

The New Slayers

Now there is a new Slayer Line, descending from Buffy and Faith through the Slayers who fought so courageously at the final Battle of the Hellmouth, when the Seal of Danthalzar opened for the last time: Kennedy, Vi, Rona, Chao-Ahn, Shannon, Caridad ... It is to them that I dedicate this Guide, and to the hundreds of Slayers we have yet to meet all over the world to whom I offer it.

With all my best wishes,
Rupert Giles,
Watcher <u>Emeritus</u>

Does that mean best? Or oldest? Or tweediest? —B

Part I
Vampires

Absalom

Absalom, one of the Master's followers, was a devout member of the Order of Aurelius. He dressed formally and quoted scripture from the writings of Aurelius. Directed by Collin, the Anointed One, he implemented the plan to resurrect the Master. Willow, Xander, and I had doused the Master's bones with holy water and buried them in sanctified ground. Vampire minions scalded their hands digging up those bones, but were ruthlessly ordered to continue. Absalom gathered the necessities for the Resurrection Ritual and spearheaded the kidnapping of the humans who were closest (physically) to the Master when he died: Willow, Cordelia, Jenny Calendar, and me. He hung us upside down and was preparing to spill our blood onto the Master's skeleton when Buffy, Angel, and Xander arrived just in the nick of time. Faithful to the end, Absalom attempted to kill the Slayer with a sledgehammer. Buffy defeated him handily, and burned him to death with a torch. Adding insult to his defeat, <u>Buffy pulverized the Master's bones with that same sledgehammer.</u>

HA! Have sledgehammer, will pummel!
—B

B ground his bones to make her bread.
—X

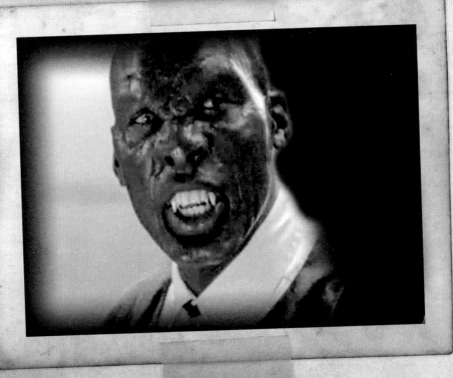

Andrew Borba

Andrew Borba was a crazed passenger preaching about God's judgment when vampires forced the bus he was on to crash. Borba, the driver, and three other riders died. Two became vampires: a boy named Collin and Borba. I believed that this was the fulfillment of a prophecy found in the writings of Aurelius: "Five shall die, and from their ashes, the Anointed shall rise." Borba's corpse was taken to the Sunnydale Funeral Home, and I was certain he was the Anointed after I read in the paper that he had been sought by the police for questioning in a double murder. Retaining his religious fervor when he rose as a vampire, Borba believed that he had been judged and found worthy of resurrection, and that God was giving him permission to suck the blood of the "chaff." When he attacked Owen Thurman, Buffy, and me in the cremation room, he was startled because my cross blocked him. Buffy took advantage and slid him into the cremation chamber, where he was destroyed.

He almost killed my date! —B

Angel's, like, my rehab sponsor.
—F

Angel/Angelus

ngel was born with the name of Liam in Galway, Ireland, in 1727, and raised as the spoiled son of a merchant. On a night of drunken whoring, he was changed into a vampire by Darla, and they became a monstrous couple that terrified the world. Ironically, in life Darla had been a prostitute herself, on the verge of dying of syphilis when the Master turned her in 1609.

Angel's little sister mistook her vampiric brother for an angel and invited him into the family home, where he massacred his entire family. The cruelty and barbarity of "Angelus, the One with the Angelic Face" are legendary. For example, he toyed with Drusilla, a young Victorian woman plagued with clairvoyance, driving her completely mad before changing her into a vampire in 1860.

In 1888, Angelus killed a beautiful Kalderash Gypsy girl, and her tribal elders cursed him by giving him back his soul. Now possessed of a conscience, Angel (no longer known as "Angelus") dwelled in perpetual anguish over the heinous acts he had committed as a vampire. He moved to New York, where, filthy and half-mad himself, he lived on rats' blood.

A demon named Whistler was sent by the Powers That Be to reclaim Angel for the side of good. When Buffy moved to Sunnydale, Angel cautiously fed her information about the Master and other nefarious villains drawn to the Hellmouth. Eventually he gave in to his feelings for her, and during their first kiss, Buffy discovered that he was a vampire ... with a soul.

I had never heard of such a creature, and I was quite vocal in my insistence that she kill him at once. But over time, Angel proved himself to be as devoted to fighting the Demons of the Hellmouth as he was to Buffy. We used the demon inside him to rid ourselves of the relentless demon Eyghon, scourge of my own rebellious youth, and Angel often gave us essential information and even saved our lives on occasion. Unfortunately, once he and Buffy consummated their relationship, the second part of the Gypsy curse took effect: if he ever experienced a moment of true happiness, he would lose his soul. In their time together, his soul was ripped from his body, and he reverted to the soulless monster Angelus.

Angelus tortured me for hours; he did everything he could to break Buffy's spirit and well as her heart; he tried to kill Willow … and he murdered my love, Jenny Calendar. Though "Janna" of the Kalderash clan hid her true purpose for being in Sunnydale—to make sure that Angel still suffered—Jenny spent her last moments perfecting the Restoration Spell that Willow eventually used to return Angel's soul to him.

It took me quite a long time to accept that his sadistic impulses had once more been restrained. And longer to stand being around him. And longer still to forgive him.

Once he and Buffy knew that they could have no real future together, Angel left Sunnydale and <u>moved to Los Angeles to atone for all his wrongs</u>. He visited us upon occasion in Sunnydale, and gave Buffy the amulet that helped us win the day at the final Battle of the Hellmouth. Now that Buffy is no longer the only Slayer, one wonders what will transpire between the two of them.

Vampires

Billy Fordham

This is one of the most tragic instances of betrayal Buffy has ever faced. "Ford" was a boy one year older than Buffy; she had known him in Los Angeles for seven years. She had an unrequited crush on him (in the fifth grade) and the affection certainly continued once he arrived in Sunnydale. He discovered that she was the Slayer shortly before she left Los Angeles, and subsequently learned that he had only six months to live because he was terminally ill with brain tumors. In Sunnydale, he created a cult of young people dressed in Goth clothes, ruffles, and capes who worshipped vampires and dreamed of becoming vampires themselves. He made contact with Spike and offered to give him the Slayer; in return, Spike would change him into a vampire. Although his terrible situation deeply moved Buffy, she could not ignore the facts: he was willing to allow the vampires to kill all his friends, including Buffy. Though Spike did in fact change him into a vampire, when he rose, Buffy immediately staked him.

"Lily" AKA "Chanterelle" and I hooked up in LA. —B

And by "hooked up" you mean ...? —X

Boone

I'm nonplussed by this turn of events: whilst masquerading as Buffy, Faith willingly abandoned her plans to take a flight out of town and returned to take on Boone and his followers. Boone was a vampire acolyte of the demon-human-robot hybrid Adam. After Adam decapitated one of Boone's followers, Boone submitted to Adam's leadership. Adam inspired Boone and the other vampires to lose their fear of religious objects. Boone led an attack on some worshipers in a church. As he strutted about, he said: "It's hard to believe. I've been avoiding this place for so many years, and it's nothing. It's nice, got the pretty windows, the pillars, lots of folks to eat ... Where's the thing I was so afraid of? You know, the Lord? He's supposed to be here—he gave us this address. Well, we'll just have to start killing off his people, and see if he shows up." I note that Faith and Buffy have switched back into their own bodies, and Faith has disappeared.

> Back again, Boss!
> —F

> Speaking of showing up, Riley was on his way in to attend the service. Sweet much?
> —B

Collin
(The Anointed One)

Collin was a young child riding in the same bus as Andrew Borba. Like Borba, he was changed into a vampire. For some time, we assumed that Andrew Borba had been the Anointed One, but Jenny Calendar and I eventually realized that the Anointed One was a child. Buffy presented herself to him, and he led her into the underground cave where the Master waited. After Buffy killed the Master, Collin spearheaded the failed campaign to revivify him. Then he decided that whoever killed the Slayer on the Night of St. Vigious would take the Master's place. Spike put himself forward, but invaded Sunnydale High on Parent-Teacher Night instead. Spike was unable to kill Buffy. Members of the Order of Aurelius declared that he must give his life in penance, but Spike turned the tables on them: he destroyed the Anointed One instead by throwing him into a cage and hoisting it up into the sunlight. The Anointed One was reduced to ashes in seconds. Think of it: after all that worry, this "Big Bad" simply went up in smoke!

OMG, Giles, are you actually developing a sense of humor? Does this mean there's gonna be another apocalypse or something?!
—B

Very funny. And may I note there is a "u" in "humour." Or rather, there should be. Except, of course, we are in the American dimension, not the civilized one.
—G

Dalton

Dalton was an unusual vampire: an intellectual with a love of reading and a gift for languages. Spike put him to work translating the du Lac manuscript, which he believed could contain a cure for Drusilla's wasting disease. When Dalton failed, Spike nearly killed him. He was saved when Drusilla realized that the manuscript was written in code, and they required the du Lac Cross to decipher it. Dalton broke into du Lac's tomb and stole the Cross. Then he successfully translated the manuscript, and Drusilla was restored. On Buffy's seventeenth birthday, she stopped him from delivering a piece of the Judge to Spike and Drusilla. Drusilla threatened to blind Dalton, but instead, Spike sent him back to retrieve the box, saying, "He's a wanker, but he's the only one we've got with half a brain." Dalton succeeded in getting back the box, which completed the construction of the demon Judge. For his pains, he was selected to serve as the Judge's first victim. The Judge burned all gentle sentimentality—traces of humanity, in other words— out of him, and he turned to ash.

OH, SURE, PICK ON THE NERD . . . —W

Darla

We modern girls prefer the term "skanky ho."
—B

Angel told us what we know about Darla. She was born in England in the early sixteenth century and migrated to the Virginia Colonies, <u>amassing a fortune as a beautiful courtesan.</u> In 1609, as she lay dying of syphilis, the Master disguised himself as a priest in order to gain access to her chamber; in his presence, she rejected God. Delighted, he transformed her into a vampire. He christened her "Darla," a variant of "Darling." By the time she met Angel she could no longer remember her original name. She changed Angel into a vampire in Galway in 1753. The besotted couple cut a swath through the British Isles; then she presented him to the Master in 1760, but Angelus ridiculed the Master's leadership of the entire Order of Aurelius and mocked the Order itself, of which Darla was a member. He and the Master came to blows and Darla was entranced by Angelus's defiance. She made her choice and left with "the Stallion," as the Master called him.

In 1860, Angelus sired Drusilla, who was then an innocent Catholic girl plagued by visions. Drusilla lamented her loneliness to "Grandmother," as she often called Darla. In 1880, Darla and Angelus encouraged Drusilla to create a companion of her own, Darla suggesting that she turn the "first drooling idiot" she came across. This was Spike.

Angel and birthdays . . . bad combo.
—X

In 1898, Darla presented Angelus with a lovely Gypsy girl <u>for his birthday.</u> He drained her dry. Her clan, the Kalderash, cursed him by returning his soul. Darla went at once to the Gypsy camp to force their leader to take it away again, without luck. During the Boxer Rebellion in China in 1900, she tested Angelus's loyalty by trying to force him to drink of a baby; he refused. She drove Angelus away, repulsed by his "filthy" soul. When the Master brought his court to Sunnydale, she attempted to seduce Angel back into the fold, but he remained loyal to Buffy. By making it appear that he had attacked Buffy's mother, her hope was that either he would kill Buffy or that Buffy would kill him. Instead, Angel staked Darla. I have been informed that Darla has been sighted in Los Angeles. I don't know how that's possible but if it's true, it's very bad news.

She tried to shoot me! What a loser vampire! —B

DEMONS OF THE HELLMOUTH

Dracula

Yes, *the* Count came to Sunnydale in search of Buffy Summers, the famous Vampire Slayer. We were all a little starstruck, even I. Anya had a tryst with him back in her Vengeance Demon days, and he and Spike had been old rivals until Dracula got famous and moved on. (He still owed Spike eleven pounds sterling.) Dracula possessed unique and, frankly, intimidating capabilities among vampires, as were described in Bram Stoker's famous novel: he could dissolve into mist and transform into a wolf and a bat. I was quite shocked, having been schooled that vampires simply could not change form.

He also possessed potent mind-control powers. He forced Xander to become his bug-devouring minion and was able to overcome Buffy's resistance to his bite. Though she attempted to hide the telltale marks on her neck, observant Riley brought her deception to light. Thus we were even more concerned about the threat he posed.

Dracula's connection to the Slayer was deep and life-changing for her; he emphasized repeatedly that they were both creatures of darkness who lived for the hunt. Buffy allowed Xander to take her to Dracula's castle. (A castle, I may add, that none of us had ever realized was in Sunnydale, and is not on any map. I believe it was enchanted, and I wonder to this day if it withstood the closure of the Hellmouth. It may be the last thing standing, though unseen to us.) In his eagerness to bend her to his will, Dracula invited Buffy to drink of him to discover her true nature. He fully intended to change her into a vampire. (What the Three Sisters who attacked me had planned, I shall never know.) She reported to me a sensation of incredible euphoria and strength, her mind blazing with images of herself on the hunt, and of The First Slayer. But this was an egotistical miscalculation on Dracula's part. Drinking his blood proved to be Buffy's ultimate weapon, granting her the power to deny him a hold on her. Freed from his thrall, she attacked and staked him. Twice. Each time, after he was dusted, he began to re-corporealize from mist. Then he shrank from the Slayer's presence. However, one assumes that he lives on . . . .

From here on, I am no one's butt monkey! Not even my dark lord's. —X

Yeah, I bet he's not bragging to his friends about his big night with the Slayer!
—B

Drusilla

That's putting it mildly. You were so stuffy your picture was in the dictionary under Taxidermy. —B

Drusilla is a fascinating case study regarding some of the things I have learned about vampirism through my years on the Hellmouth. <u>When I first came to Sunnydale, I had rather strong opinions about the proper order of things in the world of the supernatural.</u> This was a result of my family's position within the Watchers Council: I was the son and grandson of Watchers. I had been taught from an early age that vampires were soulless creatures incapable of love, and yet I was presented with the paradox of Spike's adoration of Drusilla, the vampire who sired him.

Spike rejected Drusilla when she came back to Sunnydale to claim him while we were combating Glorificus the Hellgod. I'm terribly glad that he broke her unbeating heart. —G

Before Angelus changed Drusilla, she was a devout Catholic who worried for her immortal soul because she was clairvoyant. From the French, "clairvoyant" translates as "seeing clearly": she had visions, sometimes induced by touching objects; at other times, she fell into trances. Her mother claimed this was proof of the Devil's influence in her life, a fear that Angelus encouraged her to believe while he masqueraded as a Catholic priest. Once he had twisted her poor mind into knots, he changed her, forever trapping her demonic aspect in madness.

And yet, Drusilla possesses complexities I had not been trained to expect in the vampiric undead. An insane vampire, to me, could

DEMONS OF THE HELLMOUTH

only be like Zachary Kralik, the savage monster selected to hunt Buffy during the rite of passage on her eighteenth birthday known as the Cruciamentum (a ritual, thankfully, I terminated). In point of fact, I had been taught to view all vampires as marauding beasts who gave in to their bloodlust as soon as they rose from their graves. And it is true I have seen many such creatures, with no more personality than a rabid dog.

However, it is my reconsidered opinion that there is a continuum of enduring human feeling in the bloodsucking world. Beyond leading the Order of Aurelius, the Master created a family that lasted for generations, some of whose members pledged their loyalty to him not out of fear but through real affection. Spike and Drusilla were at one time truly devoted to each other, and neither possessed souls.

Addendum: I write these words with a heavy heart. It is years later now than when I first began this entry on Drusilla, and what tragedy she has wrought! After hypnotizing me into believing I was sharing vital secrets with my dead Jenny, she mesmerized and murdered Kendra, the Vampire Slayer called to duty after the Master drowned Buffy. I now reread my previous musings with some shame. More than once, my intellectual curiosity as Watcher has distracted me from my primary duty, which is to learn everything we can use to defeat the powers of darkness. —G

Don't blame yourself, Giles. The attack on Kendra was part of Angelus's plan to send the world to hell. Some day I will send Drusilla to hell. —B

Hell's too good for her. I'll drag her to Oxnard. —X

We will send her to hell, B!
—F

The Gorch Clan
(Lyle, Tector, and Candy)

Lyle and Tector Gorch were originally gunslingers from Abilene, Texas, who made a name for themselves in 1886 by massacring an entire Mexican village. Buffy thrashed Lyle in a video game parlor in the Sunnydale Mall, and he retreated. The two cowboy brothers ambushed her in the basement of Sunnydale High, unaware that she was in the midst of attacking a mind-controlling Bezoar. After the Bezoar devoured Tector, Lyle attempted to feed Buffy to it. She survived, but Lyle told the Slayer that their vendetta was concluded, and he fled. However, he met and married Candy, and they returned to Sunnydale for SlayerFest '98, eager to hunt and kill Buffy and Faith. After knocking me out in the library, they opened up Buffy's weapons cache and waited for the two Slayers, not realizing that Cordelia, not Faith, was with Buffy. Buffy used a spatula Cordelia had found to stake Candy Gorch. Then Cordelia faced down Lyle and he retreated. We do not know where the posturing blowhard is now.

Lyle and Tector Gorch. No photograph of Candy (appalling name) exists in our possession. —G

Gotta say, Cordelia came through. —B

No, you don't gotta say! —W ☹

Harmony Kendall

Harmony was a Sunnydale High School student and a member of Cordelia's mean-spirited clique, the "Cordettes." She did fight bravely against the Mayor on Graduation Day, but we did not realize that during the fray she was changed into a vampire. She gathered and led a gang of vampires, which boggles the mind, as she retained the vapid, superficial nature she demonstrated in high school. (And one finds it difficult to imagine that her unparalleled collection of unicorn figurines would inspire confidence in the ruthless undead.) We were not particularly bothered by her presence until she allied herself with Spike, who had returned to Sunnydale to find the Gem of Amarra. She referred to him as her "blondie bear," and they separated at least twice. She gave him sanctuary after he escaped from the Initiative; this reunion did not last either. In her own campaign against Buffy, she kidnapped Dawn, but met defeat as usual at our hands. Once she realized that Spike was genuinely in love with Buffy, she left Sunnydale.

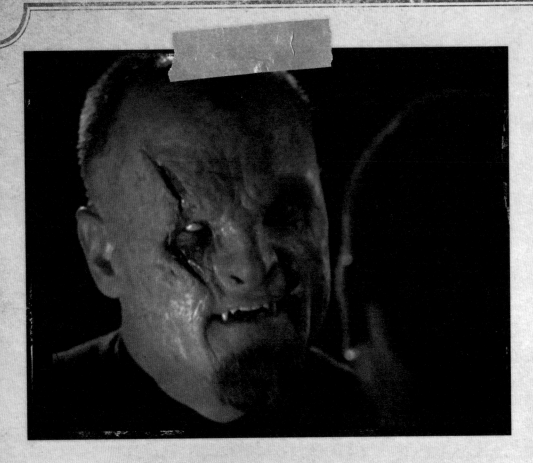

Kakistos

But sounding like "kissing toast."
—B

"Kakistos" is a Greek word meaning "the worst of the worst." He most definitely was bad news—ruthless and brutal. He was so old that his hands and feet were cloven. He had brutally murdered Faith's Watcher, and in the fracas Faith scarred him and took an eye. Then she ran, and she blamed herself for her inability to save her Watcher. Faith was so terrified of him that she hid her true reason for coming to Sunnydale—to seek Buffy's protection—and told us that her Watcher was on the annual Watchers' Retreat (to which I had, suspiciously, not been invited). Hunting Faith down, Kakistos arrived in Sunnydale with his lieutenant, Mr. Trick. Buffy joined forces with Faith and they took on Kakistos together. However, when Buffy staked him, the thickness of his ancient body prevented her stake from reaching his heart. Faith ran him through with a two-by-four, avenging her Watcher and reclaiming her confidence. The monster turned to dust.

Thanks for the assist, B! —F

Luke

Luke was the Master's devoted second-in-command. He was changed into a vampire prior to 1843, when an enemy "caught him sleeping." His strength and agility were such that only a Slayer could best him in battle. Luke watched over the Master for sixty years. When the stars aligned for the ritual of Harvest, Luke, Darla, and the Master's other vampire minions brought the Master humans to drink from in order to gather his strength. The Master chose Luke to serve as his Vessel, a position of honor requiring the highest confidence and trust. Luke was sent to the Bronze to drink from humans; each time he drank, the resulting power was magically transferred to the Master, who was on the verge of breaking free. Once unleashed, the Master would open the Hellmouth, allowing the Old Ones—pure demons—to retake the world from humans. Buffy tricked Luke into thinking the sun had risen, and while he was cowering from what turned out to be a stage light, she staked him.

Because of Luke and Darla I had to stake my best friend, Jesse.
SUCKED —X

DEMONS OF THE HELLMOUTH

The Master

Actually, French class was my first adversary. —B

The Master was Buffy's first adversary upon her arrival in Sunnydale. He was born Heinrich Joseph Nest, and when she encountered him, he was six hundred years old. He was the head of the ancient Order of Aurelius, a cult of vampires who worship the Old Ones. (We can assume that there may be other branches of the Order, and you might encounter them in other parts of the world.) The Order was dedicated to opening the Hellmouth to allow the Old Ones—the pure demons—to return to our world. They nearly succeeded in 1937, but an earthquake swallowed half the town and sealed the Master inside a buried church.

There he languished for sixty years, until the stars aligned for a ritual known as the Harvest. On this night, which comes only once a century, the Master selected a Vessel, a vampire named Luke. With each human Luke drained of blood, the Master became stronger, and was nearly able to escape his prison. However, with a small amount of help from Xander, Willow, and me, Buffy thwarted Luke, and the Master remained imprisoned.

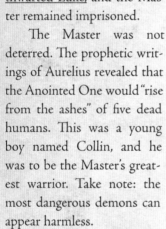

Giles, I didn't THWART him. I KILLED him. And you guys were a big help. Love you guys!

—B

The Master was not deterred. The prophetic writings of Aurelius revealed that the Anointed One would "rise from the ashes" of five dead humans. This was a young boy named Collin, and he was to be the Master's greatest warrior. Take note: the most dangerous demons can appear harmless.

The Master was just as hideous as he was dangerous, however. With his great age, his humanity had faded, and with his ghostly white,

DEMONS OF THE HELLMOUTH

Hey, Buffy, I liked your dress! —X   XO, Xand. —B

batlike features, he resembled the Turok-Han, the pure vampires we fought in the Last Battle. Aside from his preference for wearing a somewhat Nazi-like leather suit, he was also rather old-fashioned, wedded to his religion and its prophecies, and his reliance upon them ultimately resulted in his death. According to the Pergamum Codex, the Slayer was to come to him, he would kill her, and then "the stars themselves will hide" when the Hellmouth opened. It's true that he did drink Buffy's blood and then drown her. But Xander was able to revive her with CPR, and she came back the stronger for it. She was able to withstand the Master's hypnotic summons, and then *she* killed *him*. The Hellmouth closed . . . but of course, it opened again later. Several times.

The Master's death did not signal the end of our troubles with him. He did not turn to ash after he was staked. One assumes this was due to his great age and power. Although we buried his bones in consecrated ground, his followers exhumed them and attempted to revive him through another ritual involving the blood of "those closest to the Slayer." Another note: always fully destroy the bodies of magical enemies.

He also ruled in an alternate dimension wished into being by Cordelia, where he was a thoroughly modern mass murderer who loved technology. He killed the Buffy of that dimension quite handily. His minion, a vampiric Willow, was accidentally transported into our dimension. Imagine what might have happened if the Master had appeared instead! Note this well: There may be other versions of the Master in other dimensions.

HEY, SHE WAS SCARY ENOUGH! AND EVIL! AND SHE HAD . . . QUITE A CHEST! —W

You got that right, girlfriend! —F

Vampires

Spike

Rest in peace, Spike.

I am alive to write this entry because of Spike, who gave his life at the Battle of the Hellmouth. Who could ever have guessed that a vampire would wear the amulet of a true champion, and win the day against the forces of darkness?

I have learned over time that Spike was born "William Pratt," a naïve young Victorian man who lived with his mother and wrote "bloody awful" poetry (hence

he was called "William the Bloody"). Drusilla sired him while he was in a blue mood, having been rejected by the girl he loved. He is the last of a direct line linked to the Master: from Darla to Angelus, Angelus to Drusilla, and Drusilla to him. He was vicious beyond the telling, and acquired the nickname "Spike" because of his fondness for torturing people and animals with railroad spikes. He killed two Slayers in his day, a fierce and astonishing feat no other vampire has ever equaled, to my knowledge.

For a long time, when Spike was still evil, he was overshadowed by Angelus, the patriarch of their evil vampiric family, but after Angelus became ensouled, Spike and Drusilla went off on their own. Drusilla was weakened during an attack by a mob, and Spike succeeded in curing her by merging Angel's blood with hers. Later, he secretly allied himself with Buffy to stop Angelus from sending the world to hell because, actually, he rather liked our world.

He returned to Sunnydale and took up with Harmony Kendall, of all people (I mean vampires), to find the Gem of Amarra, which would render him invincible and able to walk in sunlight, and he was every bit as evil and brutal as he had

ever been. Then his life changed when he was captured by the Initiative, a secret military organization that implanted a chip in his brain that prevented him from harming humans. He became what I believe is called the "frenemy" of our side, assisting in the "ass-kicking" of demons. Though he betrayed us several times, each time gleefully reminding us that he was evil, our familiarity with him made it impossible for us to stake him. He even lived with me for a time, microwaving his blood in my favorite librarian coffee mug. He would have willingly died rather than reveal to the Hellgod Glory that Dawn was the key to reclaiming her power, and Buffy never forgot that. Nor did I.

Behold,
Giles has the
knowledge!
—G

And me! Another
plus of Hellmouth
destruction? My
parents' basement:
GONE. —X

After Willow brought Buffy back from heaven (at any rate, we assume that is where she went), the Slayer suffered a very dark period. Drinking and playing poker for kittens with Spike escalated to an unhealthy sexual relationship with the besotted vampire.

Can we not, Giles!? —B

It is remarkable to me that Spike had the capacity to feel deep love when he did not have a soul: love for his "black goddess," Drusilla, and love for the Slayer. That love filled him with remorse when he tried to force himself on Buffy, and it sent him to Africa to endure horrible trials and tortures in order to acquire a soul. That soul was for Buffy, so he could properly love her … and he, hoped, be loved by her. In the end, it allowed him to die for love … to make absolutely certain Buffy would be safe. Possessing a soul redeemed man as well as monster.

And Spike, and his soul, redeemed us.

*And I love
him for it.
—B*

Sunday

Sunday was the big vampire on campus at UC Sunnydale. She presided over a nest of vampires (Dav, Tom, Jerry, and Rookie) who stole the belongings of students, left fake notes indicating that their victims had decided to quit school, and then murdered them. I do confess that when Buffy came to me for help with Sunday, I told her to handle it herself. Her new school friend Eddie received the vampires' "I'm leaving school" treatment, and as a vampire he lured Buffy into Sunday's clutches. Sunday beat Buffy in their first encounter, cracking her arm. Next Sunday took all Buffy's things and left one of her telltale farewell notes. Buffy was terribly shaken, and Xander came to her aid. While they were spying on Sunday, Buffy was incensed to see the arrogant vampire mocking her fashion sense and reading her diary. Willow and Oz brought Buffy weapons, and in the ensuing melee, Buffy staked Sunday. Belatedly deciding to help, I arrived only in time to assist with carting Buffy's belongings back to her room.

Knew I could count on my Xander. —B

Nothin' says "thank you" like dollars in the waistband. . . kidding! —X

Mr. Trick

Mr. Trick served the ancient vampire Kakistos. He was technologically forward-thinking and pragmatic: he abandoned Kakistos when his master was outgunned by Faith and Buffy. He organized "SlayerFest '98," a hunt whose object was to kill the Slayers. At the disastrous conclusion, the Mayor brought Mr. Trick on board to help set the stage for his Ascension. The Mayor had to ensure that the rituals for his Ascension were carried out flawlessly, and that we would not be able to stop him. For example, Mr. Trick employed Ethan Rayne to create enchanted candy that changed adults who consumed it into immature teenagers. (I confess that Buffy's mother and I were both quite affected by this terrible curse.) Whilst we were … distracted, vampires stole five newborns from the hospital nursery to offer as tribute to the Demon Lurconis. I am not certain exactly what part Lurconis played in the Mayor's plans for Ascension, but the matter is moot. Mr. Trick tried and failed to kill Spike when Spike returned to Sunnydale to get a love spell from Willow. After Faith killed the Deputy Mayor, the Slayers discovered that Mr. Trick and the Mayor were in league. Mr. Trick subsequently attacked the two Slayers at the docks. He was about to choke Buffy to death with his tie, but Faith staked him and he perished.

Eeew, Giles! —B

Turok-Han

As all the Slayers who fought in the Battle of the Hellmouth are aware, the Turok-Han are (or rather, were) the "real" vampires. They were to vampires what modern-day humans are to Neanderthals. Hideous to look upon, with their bald heads, batlike faces, jutting fangs, reptilian eyes, and clawed fingers, they wore tattered leather clothing and boots. Though to every appearance nothing more than instinctive killing machines, they were sophisticated and self-aware. After The First Evil and its minions bled Spike to open the Seal of Danzalthar, a Turok-Han was released into our dimension, and Buffy and I learned (to my shock) that the Turok-Han were not merely creatures of myth. Before Willow activated the Potentials into full Slayers, the Turok-Han greatly diminished their numbers, and morale was abysmal. <u>Buffy fought a Turok-Han in front of the Potentials so they could see that it could in fact be defeated</u>. When the Seal reopened, we faced hundreds of thousands of Turok-Han—had they overrun the world, The First Evil would have won. However, by wearing the amulet that drew down the power of the sun, Spike destroyed them all.

Welcome to Thunderdome. —B

Anyone else notice that these guys looked like Principal Snyder? —X

DEMONS OF THE HELLMOUTH

Whip

Whip was the vampire who ran the "bite den" where Riley and other humans would go to be fed upon by vampires. When Buffy found Riley there, she lost complete control and burned the place down. Enraged, Whip and his lackeys attempted to kill her, but the Slayer ran all of them through with a large wooden beam. I caution you all not to simply dismiss the practice of humans willingly exchanging blood with vampires as an aberration. I wish to be delicate, but I must point out that when Buffy drank the blood of Dracula, she revealed that it was not a completely unpleasurable experience, and it gave her the strength to defeat him. Spike and Angelus, too, reveled in the exchange of blood upon their siring by Drusilla and Darla.

I must make mention as well that the fire Buffy started was in a warehouse district, and could have spread to other buildings. I fully understand why she was so angry, but all Slayers must remember that they cannot jeopardize human life unnecessarily.

Not at my best, gotta say. —B

Vampire Willow
& Vampire Xander

When Cordelia expressed a wish that "Buffy Summers had never come to Sunnydale," the Vengeance Demon Anyanka transported Cordelia to a dimension where Xander and Willow were sadistic, depraved vampire lovers and the Master ruled Sunnydale. Later, Anya enlisted our Willow to perform a spell to return there in order to reclaim her powers as a Vengeance Demon. They arranged herbs, bones, candles, and chicken feet, and called upon Eryishon, the Endless One:

The child to the mother.
The river to the sea.
Eryishon, hear my prayer.

At this point, Willow saw into the Buffy-less Sunnydale dimension, and it was so terrifying that she broke contact. They both assumed that the spell had not worked, but <u>Vamp Willow was transported into our dimension.</u> Soon she was terrorizing our Sunnydale as she had her own, and we had to get rid of her. Rather than stake her, Willow prevailed upon me to cast a spell to send her back. We succeeded, and we have never seen Vamp Willow since.

SHE WAS
DEEPLY
DISTURBING!
—W

And kinda
hot!
—X

Zachary Kralik

I n life, Kralik was tortured and possibly sexually abused by his mother, and he became a serial killer. He tortured and murdered more than a dozen young women. Apprehended, he was put into an institution for the criminally insane. A vampire found a way in and sired him, after which he escaped. Kralik resumed his atrocities, and was eventually caught by the Watchers Council. The Watchers Council chained him in a box and placed him inside the derelict Sunnydale Arms boarding house for Buffy's Cruciamentum test. He required powerful medication to keep him pain-free and somewhat lucid. He tricked Blair, a Council member, into getting too close while administering his pills. Kralik turned Blair into a vampire, Blair set him free, and together they killed Hobbs, the other Watcher guard. Then Kralik kidnapped Joyce Summers, tied her up, and took hundreds of Polaroid pictures of her, plastering them all over the walls of the house in order to unhinge Buffy. <u>Buffy tricked him into drinking holy water to swallow his pills, and he burned from within and exploded.</u>

Just say no to drugs. —B

You saved me from going through this, B. —F

Part II
Demons

Acathla

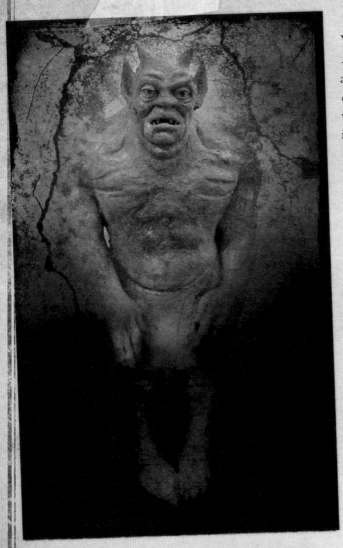

We learned about this demon from a book written by his acolyte, Lucius Temple. Acathla came into our world long ago with the intention of sucking it into hell. He was stopped when a virtuous knight stabbed him in the heart, turning him to stone. After a few misfires, Angelus discovered that the shedding of his own blood was necessary to awaken Acathla and re-create the vortex. We knew that shedding Angelus's blood a second time would close it. (This exact scenario played out when Glorificus attempted to open a portal to her hell dimension. Buffy/Dawn's blood opened the portal, and their blood also closed it.) Kendra the Vampire Slayer brought Buffy a sword blessed by the same knight, and Buffy used it to battle Angelus as Acathla awakened and the vortex expanded. Although Angel's soul was returned to him during the battle, Buffy could not spare him: she ran him through with the sword, and he was sucked into hell when the vortex closed.

Lucius Temple was also quite the gardener; he included his secret for growing heartier beets.
—G

Asphyx Demon

This is the African cave-dwelling demon Spike sought out to "make me what I was so that the Slayer can get what she deserves." I have privately wondered if what he intended to achieve was the destruction of the chip inside his brain that stopped him from harming humans. Then again, he must have known that these demons possess three powers: precognition (related to clairvoyance), the summoning of demons, and soul manipulation. If all he wanted was to get rid of the chip, why visit a demon who specializes in matters of the soul? Spike heard from the local humans that he was supposed to ask for permission to visit the demon. Of course he would have none of that. The demon tested him in terrible trials: battles to the death with a humanoid individual whose fists were covered in flame, and several other types of demons; ordeals such as bodily invasion by enormous insects and being burned and battered. In the end, Spike gained his prize: a soul.

Avilas

A group of male Sunnydale High students led by Peter Nichols worshipped Avilas, preparing to offer him a human sacrifice—fellow student Cassie Newton—in return for "infinite riches." To conjure him, they created a circle of strange coins and placed Cassie's poetry and photo in a ring of fire.

They summoned Avilas with the following spell: "Almighty Avilas, please accept our sacrifice. Appear before us, oh mighty soldier of the dark. Appear and grant us infinite riches and we will pay with our sacrifice. We kneel before you with your gift of flesh." Avilas manifested: he was immense, with huge horns, and spikes extending from various parts of his body. A strange bony protrusion extended from his jaw. He was as strong as Buffy and might have bested her, but a torch shoved into an opening in his abdomen set him ablaze. However, when Peter bent over his smoking skeleton, there was enough life force left in the demon to bite Peter quite brutally. Never assume a demon is dead. Make certain of it.

Balthazar

Back then,
a total wuss. —F

I double your "wuss" and
raise you a "chicken."
—B

Bawk!
—X

Balthazar was a morbidly obese demon forced to exist in a bath, his skin continually moistened by his followers. I must concede that Wesley knew of his cult straight off: El Eliminati, a fifteenth-century vampire dueling cult. (He was quite sure that Balthazar was dead, though—obviously he was wrong.) Balthazar declared that his enemy had crippled him one hundred years before, and that ultimate power now lay within his foe's grasp. Sunnydale was *his* to reduce to a cinder, and he would be restored and able to kill his enemy if his stolen amulet was returned to him. I'm fairly certain these comments about his enemy alluded to the Mayor. When Buffy located the amulet in the grave of a landowner named Gleaves, Balthazar used telekinesis to lift the vampires who had failed him and smother them against his body. He threatened to kill us even more horribly if we didn't hand over the amulet. Instead, Buffy electrocuted him, and we have the amulet to this day.

Clem

While Clem, a Loose-Skinned Demon, is kind and good-natured as demons go, he also cheats at poker by hiding cards in his skin flaps, and <u>he used to play for kittens, which he did devour (though apparently he has sworn them off)</u>. Before the Final Battle, Buffy asked him to reveal his hideous, tentacled true face to the Potentials as an important object lesson: that which appears harmless may actually be a lethal foe. Note that Clem and other demons in our circle have been able to "pass" among humans as people with a skin condition, or occasionally as "circus people." This ruse can be employed if you have need to protect various species of demons from discovery by the human world. Clem has been part of our lives for a long time, crashing Buffy's twenty-first birthday party, attending Anya and Xander's ill-fated wedding, crypt-sitting for Spike, and looking after Dawn. However, I would advise one to check his skin flaps before playing cards with him.

NO!
DO NOT TELL
ME HE ATE
KITTENS!
HE WAS CLEM!
—W

The Demon Children

Fairy tales can be very real. When two children were found dead in Sunnydale, fear and suspicion of witchcraft blazed through the town. I discovered a pattern: starting in Germany in 1649, the deaths of the original "Hansel and Gretel" sent their community on a witch hunt. This cycle repeated every fifty years; Buffy, Willow, and Amy Madison were rounded up by the townspeople, including their own mothers, to be burnt at the stake. I suspected demonic activity. To combat it, Cordelia and I created a potion of shredded wolfsbane, crushed satyrion root, and a toadstone. I recited the following incantation: "Ihr Goetter, ruft Euch an! Verbergt Euch nicht hinter falschen Gesichten!" ("You gods, I call upon you! Do not hide behind false faces!") When I smashed the bottle containing the potion, the "innocent" children merged into the demon that had been feeding on the town's hysteria: approximately seven feet tall, red, fanged, and hairy. Then Buffy eviscerated it with the stake her own mother had tied her to.

YOUR GERMAN WAS FLAWLESS! —W

Danke. —G

My mom's logic was cow-logic. MOO. —B

Doc

Save for a short reptilian tail that would occasionally poke out from beneath his dressing gown, blue blood, eyes that turned completely black (as demons' eyes are wont to do when they are drawing on their powers), <u>and, oh, yes, a tongue that extended perhaps ten feet</u>, Doc appeared to be a kindly older man. He lived in a pleasant bungalow filled with books and magical objects, and was known to dispense advice. When Spike took Dawn to consult him about resurrecting Joyce Summers, he was grandfatherly toward her, warning her away from trying such dark magics, then wishing her well when she could not be dissuaded. We were aghast to discover that he was actually a devoted follower of Glorificus the Hell-god, and, indeed, the portals between the dimensions might never have opened <u>had he not cut Dawn (with shallow cuts)</u> so that she began to slowly bleed. Buffy pushed him off the tower that loomed above the crackling portal and we haven't seen him since.

This is an "oh, yes?" to you? A ten-foot tongue? —B

Must you be so thorough? —B

Eyghon
(The Sleepwalker)

In my youth, I rebelled against my destiny as Watcher and fell in with Ethan Rayne and his friends, dabblers in the occult. One of us would drop into a deep sleep, and the others would summon Eyghon, a horned demon with glowing blue eyes and sharply pointed ears. The Sleepwalker could enter our dimension by taking possession of one whilst unconscious, which resulted in an incredible high. All fun and games until Eyghon would not leave Randall, who was one of us. In our attempt to exorcise Eyghon, we killed Randall. Eyghon could inhabit dead bodies, but they quickly wore out, and Eyghon swore vengeance. He tracked us by means of our identical magical tattoos—the Mark of Eyghon. Ethan destroyed his mark with acid and then tattooed Buffy as a decoy. We were able to get rid of him by tricking him into jumping into Angel (a dead body). The demon that lives inside Angel battled the Sleepwalker and, we believe, killed him.

The mark of Eyghon. —G

The First Evil

This is the most important document that I shall add to this collection. It is about The First Evil.

The First Evil claims to have existed before life itself, to have been the first of anything anywhere. It lives in the hearts of all people; it knows every form of evil in existence, every ritual to bring that evil forth. It is "the thing the darkness fears."

Every jot of malevolence and depravity across all dimensions is a part of The First. Buffy saw its demonic aspect twice, and it is entirely inhuman, with an insect-like skull and huge claws.

It took us a long time to learn exactly what it was. Buffy discovered its minions underground in a Christmas tree lot, sending manifestations to Angel of his dead victims in hopes that Angel would kill Buffy out of sheer madness. We later learned that The First Evil takes on the appearance of dead persons during encounters with the living. When Angel attempted to commit suicide, The First found this an acceptable alternative, as it would alter the balance of good and evil.

"From beneath you it devours." We heard this repeatedly, from many quarters. We knew something terrible was coming, but we did not know what. Once we, ah, detained Andrew, we cast a spell and he spoke for a Bringer we captured. (This was one of The First's

The potentials were excellently trained by the time of the final battle. A credit to Kennedy. —G

hive-mind minions—these "Harbingers of Death" were mute and their eyes were scarred shut with runic symbols.)

The Bringers' leader was Caleb, a defrocked, woman-hating serial killer. Caleb was the only human able to absorb a modicum of The First Evil's supernatural powers and healing abilities. Caleb sent the Bringers out into the world to kill all the girls in the Slayer line. He also blew up the Watchers Council headquarters in England, and I lost a number of former colleagues that day. We brought as many of the surviving girls—Potentials—to Sunnydale as we could. Faith arrived, and as you may well imagine, there was a great deal of consternation over her arrival. Everyone began arguing out of abject fear and seething resentment. Buffy was forced out of her own home, and the role of leader was awarded to Faith, with disastrous results. We nearly tore each other apart. Of course The First delighted in this chaos.

DEMONS OF THE HELLMOUTH

At the Hellmouth, The First's strategy relied on unleashing its endless army of Turok-Han—pure demons—to destroy our side and overrun the world. Buffy killed Caleb, and so The First lost its conduit to the Bringers and Turok-Han. They attacked anyway, in a thundering horde, and we fought Bringers and pure vampires in hand-to-hand combat, exposing the Turok-Han to direct sunlight, and then raining down the full power of the sun upon them through Spike's amulet.

With its army wiped out, The First had no way to continue its assault. But remember this: while we defeated The First Evil at the Battle of the Hellmouth, we did not destroy it. It gained a foothold in this dimension when Buffy was resurrected because the Slayer line was altered. *We have altered it further.*

As I have made you all aware, there is another Hellmouth in Cleveland—and I am sure more will come to our attention as you continue your missions as Slayers. Thus it is vital that you read my notes, and stay on your guard. *Evil is everywhere.* But now, thanks to Willow and Buffy, so are Vampire Slayers.

Way to go, Witchy!
Way to kick butt, slayer
Chicks! —F

WE DID IT!
—W

Time to really
live now! Tonight
we shop! —D

Party in my eye
socket! —X

Fyarl Demon

I let down my guard at the Lucky Pint with Ethan Rayne, raising a glass to the days when I had played a more important role in Buffy's life. The Slayer was nineteen then and off with Riley and the Initiative.

Ethan put something in the pint to change me into a Fyarl Demon overnight. As demons go, Fyarl are rather handsome—skin of a vibrant scarlet hue, large teeth, and a head topped with curved horns. My hooves were a bother, though, and the bony winglike protrusions from my shoulders destroyed one of my shirts.

No could understand me except Spike, who spoke Fyarl, and he also informed me that I possessed the ability to blow paralyzing mucus that would harden like stone. Buffy was about to do me in with a silver letter opener—silver being fatal to Fyarl Demons—when she looked into my eyes. She told me that no one on this earth could look as annoyed with her as I, and thus she spared me. One must take one's victories where one can.

Not sure this counts as a victory. More like a dodgy-bullety thingie. —X

Gachnar the Fear Demon

This powerful demon was summoned by an unsuspecting UC Sunnydale fraternity member preparing for a Halloween party. He painted Gachnar's Mark on the floor of his frat house as a decoration, after which Oz inadvertently spilled his blood on the Mark. This set a summoning spell in motion, and Gachnar manifested the worst fears of those in the house. He used the energy of their terror to come into our world. Spells such as these can cause a temporal flux—reality and matter distortions, which can be quite impossible to contend with unless one possesses a really good chainsaw. We located the Gaelic spell book used to copy the Mark on the floor, but we were unable to stop Gachnar's arrival. However, Gachnar proved to be so tiny that the Slayer was able to squash him beneath her shoe. The Gaelic I had failed to translate beneath his woodcut illustration read "Actual Size." A comedic ending, perhaps, but one of Gachnar's victims died and others were maimed. <u>When it comes to evil, size does not matter.</u>

Unless you want to borrow evil's clothes.
—B

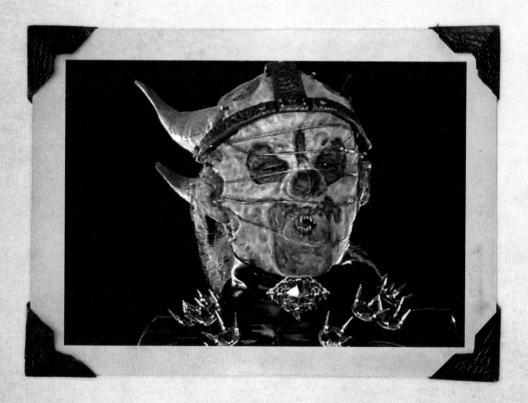

The Gentlemen

The Slayer often has prophetic dreams, and Buffy had one during a psychology lecture delivered by Maggie Walsh (which, may I say, underscores that harridan's lack of skill as a lecturer). In her dream, Buffy encountered a young girl who rather resembled Buffy herself. She was holding a box and chanting this rhyme:

"Can't even shout.
Can't even cry.
The Gentlemen are coming by.
Looking in windows,
knocking on doors . . .

They need to take seven
and they might take yours . . .
Can't call to Mom.
Can't say a word.
You're gonna die screaming
but you won't be heard."

These demonic Gentlemen, dressed in Victorian suits and possessed of excellent manners (when dealing amongst themselves), floated into Sunnydale accompanied by their capering footmen. Bald, with skeletal hands and white skull-like faces pulled into grins of metal teeth, they opened a box identical to the one in Buffy's dream and stole all the voices in Sunnydale, including Buffy's. Their footmen, every bit as terrifying with their bandaged heads and flapping straitjackets, seized the Gentlemen's victims and held them fast. Employing scalpels extracted from quaint leather physicians' bags, the Gentlemen carved out five hearts. My researches into folklore revealed that they required seven hearts. What would happen when they had all seven remains a mystery. No sword could stop them, but in one of the stories, the scream of the Princess killed them. During battle against them, Riley smashed the magical box and Buffy regained her voice. Her scream popped off their heads, the contents of which resembled a tasty lemon custard.

Sometimes I fear you. —B

These hideous beings provide us with solid proof that fairy tales are real, but the public's reaction provides even more evidence of the human mind's capacity to deny reality: television news reports described our mute condition as a result of laryngitis caused by bad flu shots!

Demons

Ghora Demon

After Joyce Summers died, we were all bereft. I've suffered many losses as a Watcher, few as wrenching. Much time has gone by, and now we are all able to remember her with some happiness mixed in with our sorrows. Enchanted chocolate allowed Joyce and me to act upon feelings that swirled beneath the surface, at least on my part.

All chocolate is enchanted! —D

"Acting on feelings" is not having sex on top of a police car! —D

Immediately after her mother's death, Dawn Summers wished to attempt a Resurrection Spell to bring her back. Sympathetic and alarmed that she should attempt such a thing without supervision, Spike took her to see the demon Doc (who would later prove to be a terrible enemy). Doc advised them to steal the egg of a Ghora Demon: "The egg of the Ghora gives life." These eggs are pink with lavender spots, and their blood glows a lovely light purple as well—a study in pastel, to be used for such dark magics. The Ghora itself, a three-headed, dragon-like cave dweller, liked to stick close to the Hellmouth. Its den was reachable via the sewer on Tracy Street. Although it was killed, there are other Ghora in the world. And for this reason, I counsel you to resist any temptation to harvest their eggs for such spells, as they can go horribly wrong.

Glargk Guhl
Kashmas'nik Demon

Summoned by Andrew Wells with a didgeridoo, this short bald demon with a waxy complexion (and a rather dramatic fringed robe) stabbed Buffy in the arm with a bony extension much like that of the Polgara Demon. The poison it injected sent her into a delusional world where she believed that she was in a mental institution and her life in Sunnydale was a manifestation of catatonic schizophrenia. Willow found a picture and description of the demon, as well as the formula for the antidote to the severe hallucinatory state. The demon's arm spine was broken and Willow brewed it with aklanate root and a handful of nettle leaves at the university laboratory. However, Buffy did not drink it, believing that the mental hospital was her true reality. Instead, she unleashed the demon in the basement with Willow, Xander, Dawn, and Tara. It was very strong and aggressive and seemed to have no language, acting only to cause mayhem. Only when it attacked Dawn did Buffy move to action: she killed it by shoving her hand into its chest. Note: It has gray blood.

And? Just as hard to get out of your clothes as red blood. —B

DEMONS OF THE HELLMOUTH

Glorificus the Hellgod

Buffy died willingly to save the world.

The look on the Slayer's face as she gave her life to save us all was serene, almost joyful. I think of the lines of a poem by Lord Dunsany, which I paraphrase here: *She liked a comet seemed, and wild and glad and free* . . .

Death was her gift.

Glorificus the Hellgod is the only foe Buffy could not defeat.

But *I* killed Glory. I had to murder an innocent, and my only regret is that I didn't do it sooner.

Words simply cannot express the despair and anguish this hellgod visited upon us. On only two other occasions have I seen my Slayer so completely unhinged: when she sent Angel to hell, and when her mother died. That is how I felt. When Buffy gave her life, I felt as though I had lost a daughter.

Quentin Travers and the Council shared one vital fact about Glory: that she was a god, and therefore impossible to kill. The two other hell-

gods she ruled with grew so terrified of her power and brutality that they defeated her in a war, then banished her to our dimension. In the same way that the Key was fashioned from Buffy's essence and sent to us as her sister Dawn, Glorificus was also concealed inside a created human being. <u>Ben Wilkinson</u>, a kind young intern at Sunnydale Memorial, came to Buffy's notice when her mother developed a brain tumor. But when Glory overtook his persona, she tortured the last monk of the Order of Dagon and members of the Knights of Byzantium in quest of her Key. To keep herself from going completely mad in our dimension, she sucked the brain-energy of her hapless victims, reducing them to incoherent, babbling mental

BEN WAS NICE. —W

Not nice enough to tell us he was Glory. —B

Demons

patients. Glory did this to our own Tara, and it was this horrible violation that started Willow down her darkest path. Those afflicted could see that Dawn was a swirling ball of green energy, and Tara blurted out the truth in Glory's presence.

It was Spike who saw that Glory was Ben. Because of a spell, it was incredibly hard for us to hold onto the knowledge that the fashion-loving, vain young woman who came into the Magic Box to buy magical supplies was the god we needed to obliterate.

Buffy and I fought bitterly over how to stop Glory. God forgive me, I told her to kill Dawn, as Dawn was the Key that would open all the portals between the dimensions if she fell into Glory's hands. Buffy simply could not do it, and I do believe she would have killed me if necessary to stop me from doing it. When Glory captured Dawn, the Slayer went into utter catatonia. Willow brought her back.

We fought Glory with the Dagon Sphere, and Olaf's Hammer, and a wrecking ball. We came at her with everything we had. A terribly wounded Glory dissolved into Ben. This was a young man who had asked Buffy out for coffee, who dreamed of being a doctor. Who promised me that he and Glory would never bother us again.

I've sworn to protect this sorry world, and sometimes that means doing what other people can't. I knew Glory would return. I knew that Ben must die, and so I suffocated him.

Writing this entry brings back all the worst memories, and I can barely stand to include it.

Glory's Minions

When Glorificus was exiled from her hell dimension, a band of her loyal minions accompanied her. We know the names of several of them: Jinx, Dreg, Murk, Slook, and Gronx. Some sort of High Priest prepared Dawn for sacrifice, but we do not know his name. They were all quite short, with black eyes and very scabby skin, and they wore brown robes. Their loyalty to Glory was unquestioned, and they were able to tell her what her human "brother" Ben was up to. Jinx seemed to serve as their leader, and Gronx was Glory's seamstress. As Glory was quite interested in her appearance, one can assume this was a position of some importance. I do not know what race of demons these "hobbits with leprosy" (to use Xander's term) were and more vexingly, I don't know what happened to them after Glory was defeated. We cannot know if they left Sunnydale, or perhaps remained nearby in hopes of returning to their home dimension. I advise caution and vigilance.

So why did she always look so skanky?! —B

Gnarl

This was the first demon we thwarted using the "Demons Demons Demons" database. Gnarl was a parasitic demon who secreted a paralyzing fluid with his hooked fingernails. He paralyzed Dawn and captured Willow. After immobilizing his victims, he would begin slicing the skin off their bodies with his nails and consuming it. He lapped up the resultant blood like a kitten. His appearance was greenish and leathery, with a grotesque hooked nose, a mouth of barbed teeth, and eyes with tiny pinprick pupils. Childlike in his sadism, he taunted his victims with singsong verses and rhymes. He was quite cruel to Willow, attempting to convince her that Buffy and Xander had deliberately walled her up in his cave because they were afraid of her. (This occurred just after I sent her home from England, and her friends had not seen her since she had flayed Warren Mears alive.)

And they were bad rhymes. Amateur! —B

BUT HE WAS A PROFESSIONAL SKIN FLAILER.—W ☹

Grimslaw Demon

These demons look like giant arachnids. They spring about on their spider-like legs and create enormous sticky webs to ensnare victims. (Apparently they also cannot be housebroken.) Once they are able to attack, they rip the heart from the victim's chest. Buffy was able to kill the Grimslaw by stabbing it with her hunga-munga.

In our case, the demon's modus operandi was quite symbolic: Anya, in her capacity as a Vengeance Demon, called up the Grimslaw to punish some fraternity boys who had tormented a young woman. That <u>Anya was capable of doing this truly tore out Xander's heart</u>. His loyalty was split right down the middle when the Slayer engaged in battle with Anya (although, as we know, Anya did not die). Slayers: there will be many occasions where you will have to weigh your humanity against your duty, as Buffy was forced to do on this occasion. I have watched Buffy weep after some of the deaths she has dealt. The Slayer's path isn't always crystal clear.

Not the funnest fun ever. —X

The Hellions
(Razor, Mag, and Klyed)

The Hellions were a <u>biker gang</u> composed of a few humans and a species of demon unknown to me who terrorized towns all over California. Their features were grotesquely stretched by means of leather straps bolted into their flesh. Once they realized that the Buffybot had replaced the real Slayer after her death, they overran Sunnydale. The amount of damage and mayhem they perpetrated is incalculable. <u>They also interrupted Willow's Resurrection Spell, intended to raise Buffy.</u> Razor was their leader, and Tara killed him by planting an axe in his back. It was the only time I ever witnessed Tara killing anything. Even though we killed most of this band, there is no reason to assume that the Hellions as a gang have ceased to exist. It may be that a vendetta exists against us in an "eye for an eye" scenario. <u>Forewarned is forearmed.</u>

You meet the nicest people on a Harley. —X

But it didn't work! Thanks, Will! —B 😊

Which is better than being four-armed! —B

UNLESS YOU NATURALLY HAVE FOUR ARMS —W 😊

The Judge

According to Angel, this ancient demon was brought to our dimension to "separate the wicked from the righteous and burn the righteous down." One may suppose this is a poetic way of saying that the Judge was intended to wipe out humanity, and indeed, he could only successfully burn to death targets who were "full of feeling," which is a human trait. He singled out Dalton—Spike and Drusilla's vampire lackey—as his first victim. I think the Judge would have been able to burn Spike and possibly Drusilla, as they were in love, but as they had resurrected him, he was subject to them. This creature was large and blue and had been disassembled, the boxes sent all over the globe. Spike and Drusilla collected the boxes and assembled him. One thing I would like to point out was that the Judge could not be killed by any weapon *forged*. We found a way around that and gave the Slayer a rocket launcher. However, the Slayer's traditional <u>hand-to-hand combat methods are still the most effective.</u>

Guns are never useful. —B

Ken

Ken was a demon who lured homeless runaway teens in Los Angeles to his fake homeless shelter, called "Family Home." He got the names of healthy teens by a complicit nurse at the local blood bank, and he preyed on their loneliness, promising them a new life if they would, essentially, be baptized and made new. In actuality, he sent them to a hell dimension where they would work until they were useless, at which point they were released back into our dimension. Time moved more slowly in our dimension, and his victims came back aged and mentally drained. Possessed of glowing red eyes, Ken also had deep bloody fissures in his head. Like the demonic slave drivers of these captive teens, he wore a black robe. His rage at Buffy for refusing to declare that she was a nobody struck a chord in her when she had ceased to find meaning in her role as Slayer. As she once told Kendra, a Slayer should use her anger to her advantage in battle.

Ken loved my impression of Gandhi . . . if Gandhi was really pissed off . . . —B

Der Kindestod

Der Kindestod" means "the Child Death." When she was eight, Buffy watched helplessly as an invisible (to her) demon killed her cousin Celia. A second chance for defeat came around to her when she was hospitalized with the flu and severe injuries inflicted by Angelus. Research revealed that only sick children could see the demon, and one may suppose that, as she was not yet eighteen, the Slayer was at the point still technically a child. She chose to infect herself with the flu virus to spike her fever. This allowed her do battle with it. A monster with its roots in folklore like the Gentlemen and the Demon Children, it was attired in a bowler hat and suit, with leathery skin, scraggly hair, an underbite of enormous teeth, and eyes ringed with red flesh. These eyes extended from their sockets and transformed into suckers that drained the life of its victims through their foreheads. A swift breaking of the neck dispatched it.

That means killed it.
—B

Demons

Kulak of the Miquot Clan

Kulak was a demon who participated in SlayerFest '98, hunting down Cordelia and Buffy during their Homecoming rivalry for the title of Queen. His skin was quite a bright yellow and he wore a sort of Mohawk triple ridge of spines atop his head. His forearms served as repositories for serrated bony weapons. He spoke excellent English and was a cordial sort to his fellow Slayer-hunters, offering to cut off the leg of one unfortunate when it was caught in a bear trap. The inefficiency of guns was once more illustrated when Buffy and Cordelia attempted to kill him with a rifle, but actually found a spatula more useful. However, it was a bomb that did him in.

This misadventure shows us that while a Slayer may attempt to mix with civilians and distract herself with trivial matters, she must protect people from the forces of darkness, not take them on limo rides into the jaws of death.

Double useful, in point of fact! We dusted Candy Gorch with it, too! —B

Homecoming Queen is TRIVIAL?! —B

Lagos

This dangerous warrior demon arrived in Sunnydale to find the Glove of Mhynegon, a gauntlet that would bestow great power upon the wearer. Wearing quasi-medieval garb, he had spotted skin and a scabbed nose, but his most notable physical attributes were his tusks and his curved horns, which resembled those of a Fyarl Demon. His reputation preceded him, such that even Angel feared him, and he defeated Faith in battle. However, Buffy beheaded him with his own axe. This serves as commentary that Slayers possess different strengths and weaknesses in battle. For example, Kendra was about precision and strategy, keeping herself centered and emotionless. Buffy uses her emotions to feed her fighting fury. Faith tends to jump into the fray, all wildness and derring-do. For this reason, different Slayers respond to different Watchers. One who did not suit was the evil ex-Watcher Gwendolyn Post, who came to Sunnydale for the sole purpose of stealing the glove of Mhynegon, attempted to trick Faith into killing Angel in order to obtain it, and died wearing it.

It's wicked fun!
—F

Beeyotch!
—F

Demons

Lei-ach Demon

I am at a loss to explain what befell the Lei-ach Demon race. They were once proud warriors, but have wound up scavenging for sustenance in the most wretched of circumstances. The Hellgod Glorificus found one lurking in the Sunnydale hospital, sucking bone marrow from the sick. Long-haired, with bone-white complexions that are covered in sores, they wear black clothing and knee-high boots. They also possess long black forked tongues. <u>Due to a spell gone awry cast by our own Tara, we were quite nearly done in by three of these Lei-ach</u> because we were unable to see them. Dawn suggested that they look like evil clowns, but apparently I don't watch the correct horror movies, for I do not see it. They can still be found skulking about, so keep an eye out for them. They can be coerced or hired for all manner of wrongdoing, including the assassination of Slayers.

Note to self: these clowns are <u>not</u> funny!
—B

POOR TARA GREW UP BELIEVING SHE WAS PART DEMON, AND SHE CAST A SPELL TO HIDE DEMONS FROM HUMAN VIEW SO WE WOULDN'T FIND OUT! —W

Lissa

I must say, it really is remarkable how many demonic women Xander has wound up with. Of course, there were also Miss Natalie French, the giant praying mantis, and Ampata, who was actually an Incan mummy, neither of whom was a demon. Perhaps one should say "nonhuman." I digress. Lissa was a demonic young woman who captivated Xander on their first date. She then captured him and dragged him to the school basement and hung him horizontally via the ropes and pulleys he had helped her purchase at the home improvement store. As she prepared to open the Seal of Danzalthar with his blood, she explained to him that when The First Evil took over the world, she wanted to be on its good side—or rather in its favor, as The First had no good side. At any rate, she had undertaken this task to prove her loyalty. Buffy decapitated her, and she returned to demon form. Although her human appearance was quite beautiful, her demonic visage was doughy and bald and covered with <u>enormous stitch-like fissures.</u>

And she seemed like such a nice girl. —X

Who was into bondage. —F

Those who do not moisturize are doomed to doughy visages —D

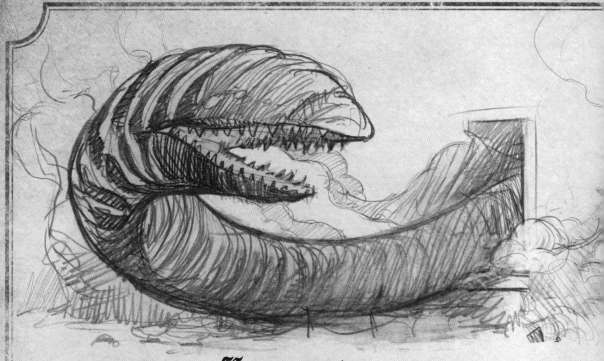

Lurconis

L urconis dwells beneath the city, filth to filth." I was able to remember that bit despite having eaten enchanted candy created by Ethan Rayne (of course.) Whilst we adults regressed back to our teenage years, Mayor Wilkins orchestrated the theft of newborn babies from the hospital. They were to serve as tribute to the snake-demon Lurconis, who dwelt in the city sewers. Buffy burned him to death with the fire from a leaky gas pipe. This was the chant the Mayor's minions used to summon Lurconis for the purpose of keeping his promise to feed the demon (I have provided a handy English translation):

Lurconis adventet. Lurconis satietur. Lurconis vetustate miliorum daemonum, novus alitus carne novorum, potens alitus precibus potentium. Lurconis hodie epuletur et clemens nobis utatur. Lurconis exsistat ut dona nostra edat illaque in carnem suam vertat. Lurconis adventet.

Lurconis come near. Lurconis be sated. Lurconis with the age of a thousand demons, kept young by the flesh of the young, kept strong by the devotions of the strong. Lurconis feast this day and treat us with mercy. Lurconis emerge to consume what we offer and make it of his flesh. Lurconis come near.

Machida

"Reptile Boy" was a giant demon worshipped by the Delta Zeta Kappa fraternity at Crest College. Half serpent and half humanoid, he appeared to his worshippers from inside a well in the basement of their fraternity. (It is quite remarkable to me how many basements there are in Sunnydale; I have learned that because of the threat of earthquakes, more modern Southern California structures lack them.) He was yellow-green in color, and his face, particularly his nose, had a snakelike appearance. His fingers were webbed, and he hissed quite a bit. On the tenth night of the tenth month he received young girls as sacrifices in exchange for money and power. Drugged at a DZK party, Buffy and Cordelia were intended to be his dinner. Part of the ritual conducted by Tom Warner, with an assist from Richard Anderson, went thusly: "For he shall rise from the depths and we shall tremble before him. He who is the source of all we inherit and all we possess. Machida!" A note: <u>Avoid socializing with strangers.</u> *Yeah, just stay home and knit, yo —F*

Cordelia tried to scream him to death. —B

Mandraz

It pains me to write of the dark days of Willow's severe addiction to magic, but my notes would not be complete without mention of Mandraz. Willow often frequented the magic den of Rack, an opportunistic warlock who offered Willow dark magics to "juice" her addiction. Only those "into the big bad" could locate his moving lair, and Willow was one of these. While there, she inadvertently summoned the Demon Mandraz, who actually looked rather genie-like (as he was described to me) with long, pointy ears, sharp features, and a nose that looked as if the flesh of his nostrils was elongated, then wrapped over the ridge. He came after Willow, who was accompanied by Dawn at the time, and Buffy took him on. One thing I should like to point out is that it was not the Slayer's might, but Willow's magic, that destroyed him. Thus it is quite useful for a Slayer to have a magic-user at her side (as long as it is one whom she can trust).

TRUST-FILLED NOW!
—W ☺

Yes, Will, you
are! —D

── 80 ──

DEMONS OF THE HELLMOUTH

Marc the Magician

Adding this after the Battle of the Hell-mouth: to a small degree, he resembled a Turok-Han. —G

This demon was the last of the Brotherhood of Seven. I've been unable to ascertain what race of demon this was, but each required a heart and a brain to retain human form for another seven years. He masqueraded as a Sunnydale High student in the absolutely appalling talent show Principal Snyder forced me to direct. Beneath his human face, he was rather typical in demonic appearance: quite spotty and scaly, with fangs and claws. Buffy successfully beheaded him with the same guillotine he used in a foiled attempt to harvest my brain. I was saved with the help of a new ally called Sid. He was a demon hunter trapped inside a ventriloquist's dummy. He ensured Marc's permanent destruction by stabbing him through the heart. It is important to note that one must not rush to judgment; firstly, I thought Sid was the demon, and secondly, we did not realize that behead-ing was insufficient to kill Marc.

We sucked! And not in a vampire way. —B

Melting Demon

Beware the power of the Wish! It is my fervent *wish* that everyone heed this plea. Magic always carries consequences. Anya's fellow Vengeance Demon Halfrek tricked Dawn into wishing that no one would leave her ever again. Shortly before Buffy's twentieth birthday, the Slayer fought a demon that wielded quite a nice sword. Red-skinned, wearing vaguely Asian clothing, he had a topknot of hair adorned with a sort of rune and spines protruding round his head. During battle with the Slayer, the demon entered his sword, and, not realizing this, Buffy brought it into the Summers' home. During Buffy's birthday party, that wish came true. No one could leave the house no matter how hard they tried. The demon materialized, nearly killing a party guest. He was able to melt into the walls, floor, and ceiling, and thus could appear nearly anywhere, rather like a household pest such as a rat or mouse, only of course far more lethal. Only by stabbing the demon with his own weapon and then breaking the weapon was the Slayer able to kill it.

How many girls get to yell "You killed my date!" twice in a lifetime? Luckily Richard survived. Just another of my fun-filled birthday celebrations! —B

Written after Buffy's resurrection: this ability to travel is quite like the demon that "hitchhiked" into our dimension when Buffy was resurrected. —G

DEMONS OF THE HELLMOUTH

M'Fashnik Demon

This race of demons has a rather ghastly hue of white and gray-green, with a reptilian snout and ridges that are gathered at the back of the head. They are a mercenary lot, hiring themselves out to perform acts of slaughter and mayhem for the highest bidder (and one is fairly certain that they do not accept kittens in payment). This M'Fashnik in particular came to my attention when he attempted to rob a bank on behalf of the Evil Trio (Warren, Jonathan, and Andrew). He came up against Buffy, and although the robbery was successful, his honor (or perhaps a simple thirst for vengeance) required that he kill the Slayer. Whilst attempting to do so, he attacked Dawn, and as usual, I was knocked out. Thrashing about for his life, he destroyed much of the Summers girls' remaining household property, as well as the house's plumbing. Slayers in particular should make certain that they insure their valuables! (And although they heal rapidly, good health care coverage is also wise.)

One pronounces "M'Fashnik"
name rather like "mmm . . . cookies," to
quote Dawn. —G

Mok'tagar Demon

Off on the adventure that is university, <u>Buffy naturally winds up rooming with a demon—"Kathy Newman."</u> Mok'tagar are shapeshifters who can travel through dimensional portals. They are humanoid, with veiny orange complexions and glowing blue eyes. They are incredibly strong, regenerate (at least, their toenails do), levitate, live a very long time, speak their own language, and lack souls. The daughter of Tapparich the Great One ran away from home and disguised herself as the human Kathy Newman so that she could attend UC Sunnydale. She began enacting the Ritual of Mok'tagar, which consisted of placing a scorpion-like insect on Buffy's abdomen and pouring animal blood in her mouth, then sucking out her soul bit by bit. Another Mok'tagar would therefore assume that the soulless Buffy, and not Kathy, was the runaway demon they were looking for. I reversed the process by burning herbs and magically supplicating the Elders of the Upper Reaches, Elders of the Lower Reaches, Elders of the Dry Lands, and Elders of the River Flats to return Buffy's soul to her.

Isn't Xander supposed to be the demon magnet?! —B

This was nothing. Try rooming with Spike. —X

Moloch the Corruptor

The first records we have of the existence of this charismatic, mesmerizing demon indicate that he was worshipped by a cult in Cortona, Italy, in 1418. He had a sort of pyramid-shaped head with downward curving horns and a skull-like nose. He was a murderous fiend who demanded that all his minions love and serve him. Some monks, led by Brother Thelonius, bound him into a book via the Circle of Kayless, and there he stayed for centuries ... until Jenny Calendar insisted that we scan the library books into "the dread machine," as I cannot help but refer to computers. Moloch was unbound and entered the Internet. Once he under-

stood what had happened, he created a false persona and made contact with Willow as Malcolm Black. He had two Sunnydale High School minions, Fritz Siegel and David Kirby, who were charged with killing the Slayer so she would not interfere with his plans to rule the world. (Fritz hanged David later when he refused to kill Buffy.) Jenny and I formed a Circle of Kayless on the Internet, forcing Moloch into a robot replica of his physical form. He almost murdered Willow because she would not declare her love for him.

MY FIRST BOYFRIEND. ☹
—W

"Disrupted"—a nice word for "I bailed out of." —X

"Old Man" Demon

THE DEMON SHOWED YOU A SCARY FUTURE. —W ☹

One of the exciting challenges of serving as a Watcher is learning about species of demons not accounted for in my books. Although I was not present at the <u>disrupted wedding of Xander and Anya,</u> Buffy and Willow described the demon to me, and yet I remain unable to classify the vengeful creature who appeared to Xander as himself as an old man. He showed Xander false images of what his future married to Anya would hold. Once unveiled, he put the blame for his deception squarely on Anya's shoulders: his name was (or had been) Stewart Burns, and she had changed him into a demon in 1914 as punishment for infidelity as a human. In appearance, he was quite tall, perhaps seven feet or greater, with an upswept angular nose and tusks protruding from his scalp like a helmet. He had taloned fingernails like D'Hoffryn's. Buffy was able to subdue him by choking him with Anya's wedding veil, after which Xander smashed his head in with a decorative column.

A scary future is working at the Double-meat Palace. Not life with my Anya. —X

Ovu Mobani

In translation, "Evil Eye" was the name of the deity that inhabited the wooden Nigerian mask Joyce Summers brought home from her gallery and hung upon the wall of her bedroom. (This might have been at the behest of the demon, as the mask was astonishingly grotesque.) Coconut-colored, it possessed large almond-shaped eyes and a mouth of heavily fanged upper teeth. The mask's eyes glowed crimson, signaling that the magical powers of Ovu Mobani were active. It began raising the dead of Sunnydale, including an odiferous desiccated cat. These violent zombies were summoned to the Summers home and killed anyone living that they could. Joyce's friend Pat was the unfortunate who donned the mask and became the demon incarnate. My research indicated that looking into her eyes induced a stunned paralysis, allowing her to come in for the kill. Buffy rammed a shovel into her face, destroying it, and all her zombie minions vanished with her. For Pat, book club was over.

I told my mom that mask was angry at the room!
—B

Polgara Demon

Known to the Initiative as Sub-T 67119 Polgara Class, Buffy and Riley pursued this demon; this species is semi-sentient, with combined humanoid and reptilian aspects, including sharp skewers they extend from their forearms when they are feeling threatened. (Note: The Glargk Guhl Kashmas'nik Demons also possess these skewers.) They have keen eyesight, a low IQ, and have to eat every two hours. Maggie Walsh and Dr. Angleman, her assistant, dissected a Polgara and transplanted its left arm to Adam.

Possibly because Adam didn't look gross enough already. —B

Later Maggie Walsh sent Buffy after two "hostiles" that she assured Buffy might be nothing but raccoons. However, she deliberately locked Buffy in with two demons the Initiative had already "collected" and experimented on, along with a defective Taser rifle. According to Buffy, these creatures looked more like they were wearing squids on their heads. Buffy electrocuted them.

Fun fact: first Sunnydale demon electro-shocked? Moloch! —B

Proserpexa, Sister of the Dark

Proserpexa is, or was, as Anya put it, "way up there in the hierarchy of she-demons" (a term which I find quite colorful). As often seems to be the case with evil creatures connected to Sunnydale, Proserpexa's worshippers sought to destroy the world. They built a narrow, pointed temple to her on Kingman's Bluff. It was covered with gargoyles and topped with symbols including a pentagram. Its most important feature, however, was the effigy of Proserpexa herself—a pink life-size humanoid female enrobed by a giant serpent, with wild, flowing hair, a forked tongue, and taloned hands. The temple was buried in 1932, during the same earthquake that also imprisoned the Master inside the church, and all her followers died. However, Dark Willow raised the temple up and, in her enraged grief, began the ritual that would focus Prosperexa's evil energies like a laser and burn the world to a crisp.

Queller Demon

Queller Demons are extraterrestrial and travel inside hollow meteors. Their history can be traced back to primitive peoples who prayed to the moon to "quell" the lunatics agitated by the moon. In the twelfth century, the Queller Impact occurred, and then the Tunguska blast happened in Russia in 1908 (the research we used had the wrong date, 1917). Although I did not know it at the time, Ben, the human vessel of Glorificus, summoned the Queller to clean up the growing inventory of people Glory had driven mad with her "brain suck" feeding technique. These bizarre "killer snot monsters from outer space" look like gigantic slugs with chitinous shells on their backs. Their white humanoid faces feature eyes ringed with black and a double row of fangs in their mouths. They kill their victims by spewing mucus over their faces, which suffocates them. One can also find evil-smelling slugs composed of protein alkaloid lodged in their throats. The Queller Demon went home with Joyce, Buffy, and Dawn whilst they awaited Joyce's brain surgery date. It terrorized the household until Buffy stabbed it dead.

I can't believe you said that! —B

I didnt. Xander did. —G

You added "from outer space." —B

Rwasundi Demon

This is a very rare type of demon, which is quite fortunate, as it is very dangerous. Its presence in our dimension creates localized temporal distortions, which are strange, unpredictable shifts back and forth in time. As we humans process time in a linear fashion, attempts by us to process these distortions result in vivid hallucinations (and a slightly tingly scalp). Three Rwasundi were summoned by Andrew Wells for the specific purpose of convincing Buffy that she had killed Warren Mears's girlfriend, Katrina Silber. And convinced she was. Anya had heard of the Rwasundi, however, and showed Buffy the relevant entry in another one of my books at the Magic Box. Of course that book has been destroyed, along with every other object in the store. But if you encounter demons covered with fissures in black robes, and possessing intense, staring eyes, arm yourselves with the realization that you are being subjected to hallucinations, and try not to panic. Knowledge is power. *And it's all about power, no?* —B

Wicked luck, B! —F

Sisterhood of Jhe

The Sisterhood of Jhe is an all-female demonic apocalypse cult. Their sole mission is to destroy the world, and in our case, they succeeded in opening the Hellmouth, however briefly. They have glowing red eyes and an abundance of hair. Their teeth are large and sharp, their ears are long and pointed, and two rows of small horns extend from just above their eye sockets to the tops of their heads. They celebrate victory by devouring their foes. We used both magics and brute strength against them, including Willow's effective revealing spell: *Obscurate nos non diutius* (Do not conceal any longer). We also conducted a binding spell from Hebron's Almanac: *Terra, vente, ignis et pluvia. Cuncta quattuor numina, vos obsecro. Defendete nos a recente malo resoluto.* (Earth, wind, fire and rain. Linger four gods, we implore you. Defend us; immediately after I will release you.) Though we closed the Hellmouth this time, ultimately our only effective weapon against the Sisterhood itself was hand-to-hand combat, and we cannot assume that we have wiped out this terrible cult.

Xand and I once celebrated in a totally different way! —F

We know. —B

Skyler

I still wonder how this demon got hold of the Books of Ascension, which the Mayor was quite eager to keep us from reading. Skyler was an ordinary sort, with the usual leathery skin, piercing eyes, long pointy ears, and a set of horns. His only unusual characteristics were his large muttonchops. He offered to give us the books for five thousand dollars, which, when you consider it, is a tiny sum compared to the actual worth of these volumes. He was quite eager to get enough money for a ticket out of Sunnydale before the Mayor Ascended. This worried me a great deal, for, at that time, we did not have a clue what the Mayor was planning. That was when the officious Wesley Wyndam-Pryce had replaced me as Watcher, and we had to have a "discussion" before Buffy was cleared to purchase the books. As a result, we weren't able to move fast enough, and when she arrived, Skyler had already been killed and the books were gone.

For Sparta!
—F

Very funny,
Faith. —G

Sluggoth Demon

We return once again to the power of the Wish. Sluggoth Demons are enormous worm-creatures that are really nothing but a mouth ringed with hideous fangs and a hollow interior for devouring large prey. Or rather, they *were*: they went extinct in our dimension around the time of the Crusades. But a young woman named Nancy lost her dog and very nearly her life to a Sluggoth as a result of Anyanka's Vengeance Demon spell. Nancy wished Ronnie, her ex-boyfriend, would become "spineless for real." Anya argued that Sluggoths *are* in the same phylum as common earthworms and that she simply "embellished." However, she caved in to pressure and reversed the spell—while Spike was battling the Sluggoth. Of course this resulted in severe injuries to Ronnie, the enchanted human. In so many of my notes one sees the repeated pattern of magics gone awry, and not just in the hands of rank amateurs. Though I hate to admit it, the Council's policy of licensing magic-users does make sense at a certain level.

GILES! ☹
—W

Suvolte Demon

These demons are non-sentient and extremely violent. They are regularly traded on the black market by terrorist groups and paramilitary organizations. They can't be trained; they can only be unleashed where total annihilation is the object. They nearly went extinct once, but they breed quickly. Seconds after hatching, the spawn become fast-moving, insectoid killing machines. When they mature into full adulthood, they are tall and scaly, appear eyeless, and have gigantic facial hoods like turkey necks filled with large sharp teeth. Their blood is a thick, gooey yellow. They can leap tall buildings. Seasoned Suvolte breeders know that it is important to keep the eggs frozen or the demons will burst from their leathery eggs and instantly begin killing. Riley Finn and his ops team (which included his wife!) were taking out nests from Paraguay on up the coast to Sunnydale. Riley discovered that Spike was the local egg dealer, and he and Buffy took the hatchlings out with grenades.

Giles has the pop culture! —B

RILEY'S WIFE REALLY WASN'T ALL THAT COOL. —W

Will, it's okay. Water over, uh, under the bridge . . . —B

Sweet

This demon told us that he has a hundred names. He is "the Lord of the Dance," "the Heart of Swing," "the Twist and Shout," and for some reason I cannot recall, we thought of him as "Sweet," though he isn't sweet at all. He is a brilliant scarlet, with a somewhat domed head and elaborate scars or striations on his face, a jewel in the center of his forehead, and a fleshy beard. His eyes are bright blue and his suit changes color from red to blue as he croons and tap dances. He compels people to sing and dance until they burn from the inside out. All of Sunnydale were affected; Buffy, Dawn, the others, and I were forced to sing about our deepest secrets and fears. Buffy nearly danced herself aflame, revealing that she had been

Isn't that some Irish guy? —B

Yes, but like Tara said: not the scary one, just the demon one. —W

pulled out of heaven by Willow's resurrection spell. <u>Tara discovered that Willow had cast a memory spell on her;</u> Spike declared his love for Buffy; and I expressed my intention to return to England so that Buffy would assume responsibility for Dawn. The terrible depression and apathy I sought to shake Buffy out of is certainly understandable when you consider that, for her, <u>returning to this dimension was the very hell from which Willow had wished to rescue her.</u> ☹

Sweet assumed he had been summoned by <u>Dawn, as she was wearing his talisman.</u> According to "the rules" she would have to accompany him to the Underworld to be his bride. But she only had taken the talisman from the Magic Box and put it on. It was actually Xander who had called Sweet forth, but he was permitted to remain with us. The entire affair had a fairy tale air, including the strange, puppetlike trio of wooden minions who kidnapped Dawn, one of whom told the Slayer she must dance for their master if she had any hope of seeing her sister again. Unfortunately, there was no happily-ever-after for us, which I'm certain was "sweet" music to this demon's ears.

My sister is a klepto! —B

Have you ever seen Angel dance? OMG. —F

My second stint as a dancer. Dollars in the waistband . . . —X

Demons

The Order of Taraka

The Order of Taraka is an organization of bounty hunters and assassins, some human and others demons. Their purpose is to sow discord and kill the unwary. They are impossible to identify save for their signet rings, which resemble a V of flames. They have existed since at least 970 BC, when King Solomon ruled Israel. Spike put a contract out on Buffy and three of the Order arrived in Sunnydale to assassinate her: Octarus, Patrice, and Mr. Pfister. <u>Drusilla's tarot deck showed them as the Cyclops, the Jaguar, and the Insect.</u> Octarus possessed one milky eye; Patrice was a stealthy predator, and Mr. Pfister fragmented into thousands of worms. Each was defeated (Mr. Pfister being immobilized in glue and stomped on), and the contract on Buffy's life was canceled. One assumes that it was canceled because once Drusilla was revived, there was no urgency to kill Buffy, a<u>nd these assassins charge quite a lot.</u> Usually, once the Order is brought into play, their members don't stop coming until their target is killed. They care for nothing else in the world but to collect their bounty, and there are plenty of the Order left in the world.

My tarot deck shows Cordelia as the evil crazy bathead.
—B

And we're not talking kittens!
—B

CAN WE NOT TALK ABOUT DEMONS EATING KITTENS ANYMORE?!
—W

Teeth

Although I suspect that "Teeth" is only this loan shark's nickname, that is the name by which I know him. Spike owed him some prime Siamese kittens for gambling debts past. (Many of the Demons of the Hellmouth, including vampires, met for poker games, at which they gambled in kittens. Cheating was common, as may be supposed when dealing with the soulless.) <u>One may suppose that Teeth was also a card shark.</u> Teeth's head was that of an actual shark, and vampire henchmen served as his "muscle." He came to collect from Spike while all of us had magical amnesia (given us by Willow) and set his vampires on us at the Magic Box. However, Buffy's natural Slayer instincts overcame her absolute ignorance about her identity, and after slaying Teeth's minions, the demon himself retreated and told Spike he forgave the debt. However, Spike was affronted and insisted he<u> was good for the kittens.</u>

OMG, Giles! You're punning! —B

Actually not so good for kittens . . .
—B

NO MORE KITTEN TALK! —W

Thaumogenesis Demons

These are demons that are created when a spell is cast. When Jonathan Levinson altered reality with an Augmentation Spell so that he could be the superstar of our dimension, he literally created a monster. Tall and hairy, with extremely long arms, the demon has a mark on its forehead of a pyramid containing several intersecting lines. This symbol revealed the demon's connection to Jonathan's magics. Though Jonathan told Buffy to fight it, weakening him, he himself destroyed it. He nearly lost his life in the process and reverted to the nebbish we knew and (mostly) loathed.   *Riley still thinks Jonathan starred in The Matrix! —B*

In another similar instance, when Willow resurrected Buffy, a destructive demon manifested and wreaked havoc. It could possess people and had a wafting ghostlike appearance. Willow used magics to make it solid, which allowed Buffy to fight it and behead it. *Gotta say, not loving the ghostliness. —B*

Other demons that travel interdimensionally include: Skaggmore Demons, Trellbane Demons, Skitterers, Large- and Small-Bone-Eaters. Although my research didn't specify which ones, it seems two of them may be invisible in this dimension, and two others can perform spells to alter perception. And one additionally drips viscous liquid.

My Jonathan collage disappeared! Tara and I made it together. —W ☹

If Xander dates one of these, I'm not inviting her over for dinner! —B

Torg

You mean demon bed buddies. —B

Torg was one of Anya's <u>former demon liaisons.</u> His long tangled hair was brown and gray, and deep swirling scars ridged his face; one scar was so ornate it resembled a seashell. He sported piercings and a nose ring. His eyes were yellow, his skin salmon-colored; he also had ritual tattoos on the bald portions of his head. Anya and I approached him in the alley behind the restaurant where he worked and asked him to create a portal so that we could request the Beljoxa's Eye to aid us in our fight against The First. He was quite unhappy to see her. He told Anya that she had broken his heart. She countered by reminding him that he didn't have one, although he did possess six spleens, two stomachs, "and half a brain, maybe." She said they'd merely both been invited to the same massacre and hooked up. I threatened him; I thought he was about to turn violent when he brandished a talon in the back of his hand, cut open his palm, and tossed his thick green blood into the alley. With these words, *"Ek'vola mok't Beljoxa do'kar,"* the portal opened.

Toth

Toth was the last of the Tothric demon clan; they were quite sophisticated, very focused, and used tools and devices to achieve their ends. He was bald with skin hanging off his face, and fissures and eyes that glowed blue-green. He wore flowing black robes. He also possessed a quite distinctive odor. Arriving at the Magic Box in search of the Slayer, he brought with him a Ferula-gemina, a tube-like weapon intended to split Buffy into two people. One of these Buffys would possess all the qualities of the Slayer, but the other would contain all her human weaknesses and attributes. He would then kill the non-Slayer Buffy, and because the two halves couldn't exist without each other, the Slayer half would die as well. This scheme was actually quite elegant in its simplicity. However, it took us some time to figure all this out.

    I attempted to beat him about the head with a statue of Oofdar, goddess of childbirth, to prevent him, but to no avail. We next encountered him in the city dump, which I surmised might be cause of his odor. He aimed the Ferula-gemina

Giles, let's not call any scheme to kill me "elegant," OK?! —B

GILES MEANS THAT HE STUNK. —W

AND SOGGY! —W

at Buffy, but accidentally split Xander in two instead. One Xander <u>was scruffy and completely lacking in confidence. The other was suave and debonair.</u> We were initially unaware of how this had come about, and along with both Xanders, at first we believed one was a demon, or possibly a robot.

Toth came at Buffy once more, and <u>Buffy dealt him a fatal stab with a sword.</u> We now knew that our two Xanders were two halves of the same person. Willow used simple magics to fuse them back together as it was their natural state, intoning "Let the spell be ended." (We shall not go into Anya's desire to find herself in an intimate situation with the two of them before they were re-fused.) As I mentioned, Toth was the last of his kind, so it is doubtful that we shall have any more duplicates among us . . .

Translation: I killed him. —B

This would have made my mom so happy: an actual normal Buffy! —B

Buffy, your mother loved you exactly as you are. She told me so herself. —G

Sometimes I miss myself. —X

Demons

Vahrall Demons

"Slick like gold and gird in moonlight, father of portents and brother to blight. Limbs with talons, eyes like knives, bane to the blameless, thief of lives." A sort of grayish-green, with insignia on their foreheads, these demons are approximately three meters tall and weigh roughly one hundred to one hundred twenty kilograms. Three of them sought to end the world employing an ancient ritual called the Sacrifice of Three, for which they required three objects: the blood of a man, the bones of a child, and the Word of Valios. Turns out I owned the Word of Valios, a talisman I purchased at a sorcerer's estate sale. They knocked me out (of course) and took it. They themselves were the Sacrifice of Three, as they intended to jump into the Hellmouth with the required objects. All three did manage to make it in, but Buffy went down in after the third one. She was able to retrieve and kill it, thus invalidating their ritual. And once again, the Apocalypse was averted.

See, Giles, shopping can save the world!
—B

GRRRRR! ARRGH!

Vengeance Demons

D'Hoffryn is the ruler of the hell dimension Arashmaharr. Stately and bearded, he has double horns and pointy ears, and wears elegant robes. He seeks out women who have cursed other humans for wrongs committed against them. He invites them to become Vengeance Demons—immortals who wield the power of the Wish on behalf of other humans who have been victimized—the dying and neglected, abused children, <u>wronged women</u>, scorned men. He even offered

Yo, some guy dumps me, I deal payback, too. —F

Willow such a life when she was left reeling by the desertion of her beloved werewolf boyfriend, Oz.

Vengeance Demons offer an ear to someone in the throes of anger or pain, waiting to pounce on the magic words "I wish." They then change into their wrinkly- or rotting-skin appearance in order to fulfill the Wish, often "embellishing" in order to enhance their reputations (and because they like doing it).

I have been acquainted with two Vengeance Demons: Anyanka and Halfrek. Over a thousand years ago, Anyanka was once known as Aud, and she lived with her lover Olaf in Sweden. When she found out that he had been unfaithful, she changed him into a troll. Impressed, D'Hoffryn made her a Vengeance Demon. Her source of power was a pendant, which the Giles of another dimension broke, rendering her mortal. She became Anya, my eventual partner at the Magic Box. She was lured back to her Vengeance Demon duties after Xander left her at the altar, but found she hadn't the stomach for it. She had two human names: as Anya Emerson, she posed as a Sunnydale High student; then she became Anya Christina Emmanuella Jenkins. She died at the Battle of the Hellmouth.

Halfrek was a close friend of Anyanka, who may have known Spike when he was the human poet William (I am not sure). When Anyanka asked to take back a curse, D'Hoffryn reminded her that the cost was the life and soul of a Vengeance Demon. She was willing to give up her own life, but he destroyed Halfrek instead so that Anya would live to suffer.

Andrew told us she saved his life.
—B

That was my girl, always doing the stupid thing.
—X

I'm sorry Xander.
—B

ME TOO
—W
☹

Demons

Whistler

Giles,
I am
shocked!
—B

Whistler is an unusual demon: appearing in human form (in appalling clothing, I must say, but one would sound superficial if one said so), he approached both Buffy and Angel as an agent of the Powers That Be. Thus he is in no way evil. He believed that Angel was destined to stop Acathla from destroying the world, and so he drove the half-mad, repentant ensouled vampire to Los Angeles to witness Buffy's call to become the Slayer. Angel felt for her, and declared that he wanted to be good and to help her. Whistler was surprised when Angel turned into Angelus and plotted to do exactly what Whistler believed he had been put on earth to prevent: release Acathla.

Whistler next appeared to Buffy. He told her that she had to be ready to do more than simply fight Angelus if she wanted to prevent the apocalypse. Armed with this grim knowledge, Buffy did the right thing, horrible though it was for her.

It really was, Giles. I loved Angel with all my soul. And he's still in my heart. —B

Dude who dresses like that has to be evil.
—F

Wig Lady

This hideous creature posed as a sweet old dear who came to the Double-meat Palace for a daily apple pie and coffee. Buffy's investigations into missing employees yielded the unappetizing revelation that they wound up in the meat grinder. However, they were not being ground into Doublemeat patties, but being devoured by the old lady. Her wig hid a bald head from which an enormous stalk could extend, topped by a bulbous monstrosity that sprayed paralyzing liquid at her prey. Unable to move, her victims were forced to endure being eaten alive. Willow cut off the stalk and ground it to bits. I have not been able to discover what sort of demon she was, and I'd guess there are more of her kind.

Doublemeat is double sweet! NOT! —B

OCCASIONALLY I HAVE BEEN KNOWN TO BE CALLOUS AND STRANGE . . . —W

Part III
Other Forces
of Darkness

Adam

I'm writing this journal entry shortly after awakening from an unsettling dream. We went back to Buffy's house after defeating Adam, and my dream seemed to center around Spike being my son, an attack from the First Slayer, and … cheese. Pay attention to your dreams; after all, the secret to defeating Adam came about through a magic spell that utterly changed our world … for a brief time. But I'm getting ahead of myself.

During her freshman year at UC Sunnydale, Buffy learned about the existence of a vast underground military operation called "The Initiative." Dr. Maggie Walsh was the civilian scientist in charge, and her secret agenda was to create a new race of super soldiers from parts of demons, humans, and machines. Her prototype was named Adam.

Adam murdered Dr. Walsh and tried to understand who and what he was, much like the monster of Dr. Frankenstein. He eviscerated humans, vampires, and demons in his quest. Eventually he discovered Dr. Walsh's research and began plotting a huge battle between humans and demons: he wanted lots of corpses in order to create more hybrids like himself.

During this time, Buffy and her friends were quite estranged from one another (I as well, I do admit). Adam took advantage of the situation to keep us from comparing notes, and as a result, we made little progress against him.

Jonathan Levinson cast a spell in which he became the "superstar" of our dimension. He was everything to us—a massive celebrity, a demon fighter whose sidekick was the Slayer, and a consultant to the Initiative. Jonathan casually revealed the vital information that we needed to defeat Adam: inside the demon hybrid's body, a reservoir of uranium 235 could power him forever.

Xander, Willow, and I performed an ancient Sumerian enjoining spell that merged our essences with that of the Slayer. With supernatural power previously unavailable to her, Buffy ripped the core of uranium 235 from Adam's chest. We then joined the military in defeating his demon and vampire followers.

But the point that continues to haunt me is that Jonathan learned the secret of Adam's power source during a manufactured reality. The lesson, then: <u>Do not discount information that comes to you in magical ways. It may save your life.</u>

Other Forces of Darkness

Ampata Gutierrez
(Inca Mummy Girl)

We knew Ampata Gutierrez as the mummy of a beautiful sixteen-year-old Incan "princess," who was buried alive as a sacrifice to the mountain god Sebancaya five hundred years ago. Ampata was originally on exhibit in the Sunnydale museum, and a cursed seal in her tomb served as a warning not to revive her. A <u>Sunnydale student broke the seal and, for his trouble, became the mummy's first victim.</u> She literally sucked the life out of him and left him a shriveled mummy in her tomb. Next, the princess killed the actual foreign exchange student whose name was Ampata Gutierrez and assumed his name. A Peruvian warrior attempting to stop her also died at her hands. She almost killed Xander, but hesitated because of her feelings for him. That was when Buffy destroyed this unfortunate Incan mummy girl. Buffy felt for Ampata's unjust fate, but would never cause the death of another so that she herself might live. Two "Chosen Ones": one a hero, the other a desperate victim.

RODNEY MUNSON! I WAS TUTORING HIM! —W

He died before he could flunk chemistry. Why didn't I think of that?!? —B

Suck face much? Seriously, I felt sorry for her. —B

Beljoxa's Eye

Anya and I consulted this oracle, which lives in a dark dimension or "external vortex" (a dark dimension) that can only be accessed by a demon. In this case, we went to Torg, a demon with whom <u>Anya was acquainted.</u> This being is a large, floating cycloptic creature—a sort of eye stem covered by many other eyes of several sizes, protected by spherical metal plates that are suspended above and below by chains. It informed us that it "sees not the future—only the truth of the now and before." Anya argued that's actually what memory is. But the Eye did actually "see" the truth regarding The First Evil: it had remained dormant for some time, but the mystical forces surrounding the Slayer line had become irreparably changed, unstable, and open to attack by The First Evil. Unfortunately, this occurred because Willow resurrected Buffy, compromising the Slayer line. One cannot be sorry for that, but we are reminded that we ought not alter the natural order of things.

ANYA
REALLY
HELPED US
A LOT!
—W

Bezoar

This parasitic, prehistoric creature dwelled beneath the original Sunnydale High School. Mr. Whitmore, the health teacher, distributed the Bezoar's eggs, which looked exactly like white hen's eggs, to Sunnydale students including Buffy, Xander, Willow, and Cordelia, for an experiment in parenting. The eggs symbolized their own human offspring, and they were to care for them. The eggs cracked open while the students were sleeping and extended mandibles into the nervous systems of their hosts (including Joyce and me, I'm afraid), which made us quite sluggish and zapped us of our free will. At this point Buffy killed hers. Xander hard-boiled his—a lucky break, as, like Buffy, he retained his free will. For the rest of us, the Bezoar young continued to grow, looking quite monstrous, like splayed chicken breasts with some modifications. Through them, the mother Bezoar controlled us and we continued to harvest and distribute her eggs. Buffy entered the bowels of the Bezoar, and when she killed it, we were all released from our thrall.

I slayed my little Eggbert, just like I killed my Gigapet. —B

Except for his weird obsession with Cordelia! —B

Bringers
(Harbingers of Death)

These quasi-demonic beings are minions of The First Evil. Blind and mute, they appeared human, with large runes carved deeply over their closed eyelids down their cheeks. They operate as a hive mind, referring to themselves as "The We." Buffy first encountered them in December 1998 at a Christmas tree lot. Willy the Snitch told her that some of the supernatural inhabitants of Sunnydale were so frightened of the Bringers that they left town. Their purpose at that time was to draw Angel to The First Evil's side in the impending final battle. When Buffy fought the Bringers, The First appeared to her in what we assume is its true form. In 2002, Caleb sent them to kill as many Potentials and their Watchers as they could locate. The Seal of Danzalthar aided in turning Sunnydale students into new Bringers, swelling their ranks. The Bringers also located the Scythe. As The First has only been thwarted, not destroyed, we may anticipate that Bringers still pose a threat.

This is a transcription of a Bringer's description of The We, spoken through Andrew Wells: "I am a drone in the mind that is evil ... I am a part of the Great Darkness; I am only a fragment of The We. We work as one to serve The First." —G

Caleb

aleb was an insane defrocked minister and serial killer who served The First Evil. The First imbued him with superhuman strength and stamina, causing his eyes and blood to blacken. He orchestrated the worldwide killing of the Potentials and their Watchers and blew up the Watchers Council headquarters in London. He also attempted to have Faith Lehane murdered in prison <u>but luckily failed.</u>

You can say that again, yo. —F

He searched for the Scythe, following a lead to a Catholic mission in the California town of Gilroy. There he discovered a secret room containing this inscription: "It is not for thee; it is for her alone to wield." Enraged, he arrived in Sunnydale and set up camp at the local vineyard. Attempts to take him out were disastrous, resulting in many deaths and the loss of Xander's left eye. In the end, Buffy sliced him in half with the Scythe. The First used his visage to taunt her after Caleb's death and inadvertently inspired the plan that won us victory in the Battle of the Hellmouth.

So glad you killed him, Buffy! —X

You and me both, Xander. —F

Cobra Monster

This giant cobra creature was manifested through an ancient Egyptian transmogrification spell created by the Temple of Sobek and Khul, their high priest. Glory's minions gave the spell to her as a gift. Glory actually came into the Magic Box to purchase items that she needed to cast it: a Khul's Amulet and a Sobekian Bloodstone. The Khul's Amulet is a transmogrification conduit, which turns one living thing into another living thing. In this case, a normal-size cobra became the monstrous cobra. After placing the amulet and bloodstone into an urn, Dreg and Glory performed the incantation in both ancient Arabic and English, which was quite lengthy. I include here a few key phrases: "From the mud, from the rot, arise, holy serpent, and be bathed, cleansed in the shadow of Sobek ... Sobek, grant the power, that it may mold this wretched creature, that it may be reborn, that it may serve—" It did find Dawn, but Buffy was able to kill it before it revealed Dawn's identity to Glory.

This was when we found out that Mom was sick. —B

Yes. I remember. Such awful timing. —G

At least I had something I could kill. —B

— 119 —

Other Forces of Darkness

Dark Willow

YOU REALLY NEED TO, GILES. IF IT DOESN'T HAPPEN TO ME AGAIN, IT MIGHT HAPPEN TO SOMEONE ELSE —W

It pains me to write this entry about Willow's descent into the blackest of magics. Willow began to explore magics after the death of Jenny Calendar. She performed a successful Restoration Spell on Angelus. At university she met her dear love, Tara Maclay, a witch, and they explored magics together. Willow quickly surpassed Tara, who began to worry that Willow was using too much magic.

I was horrified to learn that she had used a Resurrection Spell to raise Buffy from the dead. Anya procured the only Urn of Osiris from a desert gnome in Cairo on eBay and Willow sacrificed a young doe, cutting out her heart and smearing herself with the blood. Then she called upon Osiris with the time-honored incantation: "Osiris! Here lies the warrior of the people. Let her cross over." And as we know, it was successful.

After Willow "de-ratted" Amy Madison, Amy introduced her to Rack, her magic dealer. But Willow fought her addiction and Tara returned to her. As we know … I can barely force myself to write the words. Warren Mears shot Tara. Willow called upon Osiris again, but he refused to aid her. This was a "natural death," inflicted by a human onto another human.

Willow broke then, and I understand her rage completely. After Angelus murdered Jenny, I went straight to the factory where he lived with Drusilla and Spike, and I would have gladly died if I could have killed him first. Willow absorbed all my books on the Dark Arts and flayed Warren alive. She sucked magical force from Rack … and from me. I returned from England dosed with the powerful magics of the Coven who would later aid Willow in her rehabilitation. Willow nearly killed me, but the magics she drew from me transformed her rage into pain. Unfortunately, in her distress, she decided to end the world rather than endure such suffering. She would have, too, but for Xander's brave declaration of love.

Willow, after what you accomplished at the Battle of the Hellmouth, I simply cannot accept that this will ever happen to you again. —G

☹ ADONAI, HELOMI, PINE. COME FORWARD, BLESSED ONE … —W

MY HAIR TURNED BLACK AND I GOT ALL VEINY —W

ALTHENEA AND THE OTHERS HELPED US FIND POTENTIALS, TOO —W ☺

THE YELLOW CRAYON! —W ☺

Other Forces of Darkness

Ethan Rayne

Oh, Ethan, how you vex and confound me. You are far more bad than good, and yet I repeatedly let down my guard around you, always to my detriment. Perhaps separating good from evil was easier in an earlier time than ours. Based on the Watchers' Diaries, one would assume so. We found ourselves unable to stake Spike once he was chipped, rationalizing that he was harmless although we knew he really wasn't. What of that? We show no mercy to other incapacitated foes, seizing on the advantage to be rid of them. So it is with Ethan: I know him well, and though he has done terrible things, I retain a strained fondness for him. After the summoning of Eyghon in our youth, the aftermath (Randall's death) so shocked me that I returned

Remember
Giles:
BEER
BAD!
Especially
with Ethan.
—B

to the Watcher fold, and sought to become as good a Watcher as my grandmother and my father were. Perhaps that is why I was so impatient with Buffy when I first met her. <u>I had had to put away childish things; why could she not as well?</u> Ethan chose a darker path, worshipping chaos, freer in many ways than I could ever hope to be. One must concede that he became a powerful sorcerer. Once my friend, I suppose I should call him my nemesis. He has come against us a number of times, for financial gain, to please the god Janus, or to save his own skin. Yet he did warn me that the demonic world was afraid of the Initiative, and of Room 314 in particular. I've no doubt he will remain chaos's "faithful, degenerate son," and <u>that once he escapes the military "rehabilitation" facility in the Nevada desert (which he will certainly do)</u>, he will wreak havoc upon the world once more. Perhaps it is simply nostalgia for my youth that softens my stance toward him. The rest of you may thankfully be free of my bias and resist trusting him.

Possibly
because
I was still
a child?!
—B

Note to
self: road
trip to
Nevada?
—B

It was cuz of him I have
soldier knowledge. —X

CORDELIA SAID YOU TOLD HER
SOMETHING ABOUT LINOLEUM.
—W

Lock and load,
baby! —F

Faith Lehane

On occasion, Faith has been called "the Dark Slayer." So many factors worked against her: her mother was a neglectful alcoholic, and she didn't even complete high school. She carried a terrible psychic burden from having witnessed Kakistos deal her Watcher an unspeakable, agonizing death. She arrived in Sunnydale to seek Buffy's protection but did not trust us enough to share this information. Instead she charmed Buffy's friends and sparked a bit of jealousy in our Slayer.

Suffering from post-traumatic stress disorder, Faith encouraged Buffy to behave as if they owned the town. They were arrested by the police but escaped, and then Faith inadvertently staked Allan Finch, the Deputy Mayor. (I believe he was coming to the Slayers to warn them about the Mayor. What a sad end.) She sank the body in the harbor, then attempted to pin the murder on Buffy. She spiraled even farther out of control, nearly killing Xander when he attempted to comfort her.

Wesley sent Slayer Special Ops after her, and it was all over. She turned to the Mayor and served as his spy and assassin. She killed demons and humans alike. Once we realized she had switched sides, we extracted as much information as we could, and then she was utterly lost to us. When she shot Angel with a poisoned arrow and we knew the only antidote was the blood of a Slayer, Buffy nearly killed her. Then *Buffy* was nearly lost to us.

The deceased Mayor left Faith a magical device that allowed her to switch bodies with Buffy, and she experienced the love and respect Buffy has known. It unnerved her, but I believe it set her on the right path. She took out Boone and his minions in the church, sought redemption with Angel, fought with us at the Battle of the Hellmouth, and is with us now. And we are glad of it.

Giles, she was Single White Female-ing me! Moving in on my life. And my french fries! —B

Thanks, Giles! Didn't know you cared! —F

Yes, you did. —B

Other Forces of Darkness

Going Dark

Hey Slayer Chicks, let me give it to you straight about all the power that you have now. It can make you crazy. It can make you think that there's *nothing* you can't do and no one who can stop you from doing it. Can't lie that no way did I know Allan Finch was human when I staked him. But when I knew I'd taken a life . . . sounds bad, but along with the shock I felt a *zing*. A rush. Maybe that's the demon part inside each Slayer. 'Cause that's how vamps feel, you know. That's why Angel has to be so careful. So do you. We are not goddesses. We can't deal in human life. 'Cause that makes us *total* demons. Peace out.

Faith

The Geek Trio
(The Trio)

Our arch-nemesis-sis-sis.
NOT!
—X

Ionathan Levinson, Andrew Wells, Warren Mears. These three young men (if such specimens of arrested development may be referred to as "men") plagued the Slayer and caused heartbreak, madness, and death. At first "the Geek Trio" were oafish and benign, living in the basement at Warren's house with their treasure troves of superhero comic books and action figures, their speech peppered with even more references to popular culture than that of Buffy and her friends.

Each of the three had developed a specialized skill that augmented those of the other two: Jonathan was a spellcaster, who performed many spells with the use of his "magic bone." Andrew could summon demons (his flying monkeys ruined the school play). The first indication we had of Warren's technological genius was when his robot creation, April, nearly killed Katrina, his human girlfriend, in a jealous rage.

Their first forays into mischief resulted in a freeze ray, a time-distorting device, and an invisibility weapon employed in their bid to "take over Sunnydale" as crime lords. But things took a very dark turn indeed when Warren murdered Katrina. Andrew summoned Rwasundi Demons, whose very presence distorts time, and convinced Buffy that she herself had killed Katrina in the woods while battling the demons. After this, Warren asserted himself as the leader of the Trio. Andrew, the most weak-willed of the three, became his lieutenant, and Jonathan was the closest

thing they had to a moral compass. Jonathan was increasingly uncomfortable with Warren's malevolent vendetta against Buffy, and Warren and Andrew plotted in secret to make him their scapegoat.

The three stole the Orbs of Nezzla'Khan, which Warren used to become invincible, and commenced to do ultimate battle with the Slayer. Though Buffy destroyed the Orbs (after a tip from Jonathan), Warren escaped.

Then Warren committed the most heinous act of all: he shot at Buffy with a gun, intending to kill her, and in that act, he succeeded in killing Tara instead.

Utterly consumed by grief and rage, Dark Willow came after the Trio. We helped Jonathan and Andrew escape to Mexico, as she was intent on killing them, and of course we could not allow that.

Warren was not so lucky. Willow tortured him and then flayed him alive; after that, she was lost to us for a long time. But take heed, Slayers: though we assumed that Willow had killed him, I have observed magical portents indicating that Warren may be alive in some fashion, although I do not know in what form. I also do not know whom it may have been who saved him. But he may pose a threat to you in the future.

As for Andrew and Jonathan: The First Evil appeared to Andrew in the form of Warren and convinced Andrew to lure Jonathan into the basement of the rebuilt <u>Sunnydale High School</u>. Andrew stabbed Jonathan, killing him. Jonathan's blood fed the Seal of Danzalthar, which should have opened the Hellmouth. However, Jonathan was anemic, and his blood did not work. The ineptitude of these three never ceased to astonish me, but I remain eternally grateful for it.

A rehabilitated Willow spied Andrew on the street and <u>dragged him to Buffy's house.</u> He became an ally, and fought (and survived) the Final Battle. He told Xander that Anya died protecting him in the fray, but that was a kind lie—Andrew is quite a storyteller. He is still among us, and I say in all seriousness that he may be counted upon to advise and help you.

This is why going to school is bad. —F

HE WANTED TO BE OUR GUEST-AGE, NOT OUR HOSTAGE. —W

Hus

Hus was an avenging spirit warrior of the Chumash Native American tribe. He was bound inside the Sunnydale mission, which had been buried by an earthquake, much like the ruined church in which the Master was imprisoned. Freed when Xander fell into the mission, he resumed "carving out justice" by reenacting the terrible atrocities visited upon his people by the European colonials—I mean, "settlers." He murdered two people and took an ear each, then infected Xander with syphilis. He could turn into a green mist, a flock of crows, a coyote, and a bear. He called up more spirit warriors by placing traditional weapons on the floor of the mission and reciting this incantation: "First people who dwell in Mishu-pashup, hear me and descend. Walk with me upon Itiashup again. Hear me also, Nunashush. Spirits from below, creatures of the night, take human form and join the battle. Bring me my revenge." Buffy vanquished him by stabbing him with his own knife. I don't know if he's still a threat.

I'm still a threat to anyone who ruins my Thanksgiving dinner! —B

I STILL SAY THANKSGIVING IS A SHAM WITH YAMS. —W

Other Forces of Darkness

The Madison Witches
(Amy and Her Mother Catherine)

The Madison witches serve as a cautionary tale to those who would explore magics. Catherine Madison, the mother, selfishly exchanged bodies with her young daughter, Amy, and nearly killed Buffy with a Bloodstone Vengeance Spell. To stop her, I cast my very first spell as Watcher, appealing to Gilail and Corsheth (and I was very glad for the dissection frog whose eyes I used). Catherine's counterspell to Corsheth alone was cast back at her when she looked into a mirror, and it sent her to "the dark place." One assumes that would be a hell dimension, but I do recall Oz once mentioning that the eyes of a certain cheerleading trophy amongst the school's awards seemed to follow him wherever he went. Amy began using magics to avoid doing homework, and the love spell she cast for Xander backfired utterly. She called on Hecate to turn her into a rat to escape burning at the stake, and

That love spell nearly killed me! —X

BUFFY'S MOM NEARLY KILLED YOU! —W

it took Willow three years to restore her. She became a magics addict and dragged Willow down with her. Once Dark Willow began her recovery, Amy hexed her with a Penance Malediction out of sheer jealousy and spite. Amy's whereabouts are unknown, and she is not our friend.

I TURNED INTO WARREN! I NEARLY KILLED KENNEDY! —W

The Mayor

Mayor Richard Wilkins III was also Mayor Richard Wilkins Senior *and* Junior. He was responsible for founding the town of Sunnydale on top of the Hellmouth in 1899, and he spent a century paying tribute to various demons in return for power and long life. In daily life, he was very much a 1950s-style American politician who would not permit swearing in his presence and espoused family values, but behind the scenes, he orchestrated such catastrophes as the night we adults all ate magical band candy and reverted to our teenage selves so that he could steal five infants from the hospital and sacrifice them to Lurconis. (We stopped him, thankfully.) Principal Snyder kept tabs on Buffy for him, although we don't believe that

Other Forces of Darkness

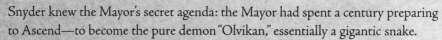

Snyder knew the Mayor's secret agenda: the Mayor had spent a century preparing to Ascend—to become the pure demon "Olvikan," essentially a gigantic snake.

This realization was made all the easier after a betrayal in our midst. Faith the Vampire Slayer arrived in Sunnydale after her own Watcher was murdered. I was replaced by Watcher Wesley Wyndam-Pryce because I had "a father's love" for my Slayer (Buffy) and Wesley became the Watcher for both Slayers. Faith chafed under his regimental approach, and one night while she and Buffy were out rebel-

ling, Faith accidentally killed Allan Finch, the Deputy Mayor. Buffy was shocked to her core when Faith refused to take responsibility for the death, and Faith began a downward spiral that prompted her to offer her services to the Mayor.

The Mayor loved Faith with the same fatherly affection I still hold for Buffy. Although he used her as an assassin (even attempting to fatally poison Angel), he provided for her and protected her beyond the grave after we destroyed him. He gave her a sense of self-esteem that we, sadly, did not.

Don't beat yourself up, Giles. We're five by five now. —F

The Mayor married Edna Mae in 1903 and she died cursing him for retaining his youth while she withered and fell into dementia. He held his own experience up to Buffy and Angel as they sought to maintain their relationship, and he opened their eyes to the impossibility of a happily-ever-after for them. He delivered death threats to us in the most pleasant of tones, and I know that he would have killed Willow had we not handed over the Box of Gavrok containing the hideous spider-creatures he had to ingest to become invincible for the one hundred days prior to his Ascension.

Prophetic dreams are one of the gifts bestowed upon Slayers. Faith appeared to Buffy in a dream and told her to appeal to the Mayor's weakness: his love for Faith. After he changed into Olvikan, he was no longer invincible, and that was the moment to strike. Buffy taunted him, reminding him that she had stabbed Faith with the very knife he had given his Slayer as a gift. Enraged, he came after Buffy . . . and we blew him to bits by seeding my poor library with explosives. You may find it useful to rally non-Slayers to your cause. Under Buffy's command, the entire graduating class of Sunnydale High battled the Mayor and his vampiric bodyguards with flamethrowers, battle axes, spear guns, crossbows, holy water, and stakes, and they carried the day.

Talk about school spirit! —B

YOUR SOLDIER SKILLS CAME IN HANDY, XANDER! —W

Natalie French

It has become something of a sad joke that Xander attracts monstrous and demonic females of all sorts, and Miss French was his first. She was another example of folklore made real. A She-Mantis, she was a variety of Kleptes-Virgo, or virgin thief. Greek sirens and Celtic sea-maidens are also of this class. She released powerful pheromones that attracted Buffy's male schoolmates, including Sunnydale student Blayne Moll and our own Xander. She may also have mated with Dr. Gregory, the biology teacher, but I can't be sure. Able to turn her head one hundred and eighty degrees, she was also possessed of superstrength. She was so dangerous that even vampires feared her. I rang up my old friend Dr. Ferris Carlyle, who had transcribed a pre-Germanic manuscript that described this creature. He went hunting after she murdered some boys in the Cotswolds, and he wound up in an insane asylum. Using bat sonar, insect spray, and a sharp machete, Buffy hacked her to death. Xander destroyed her eggs.

I don't suppose helping Xand cheat on our insect quiz had anything to do with that "attraction"!
—B

A full-on Exorcist twist!
—B

Olaf the Troll God

Olaf was once Anya's human lover in Sjornjost, Sweden, in 860. He proved unfaithful and she used a Thorton's Hope curse on him, turning him into a troll. Note: she used eelsbane for the troll element, an improvisation that quite impressed D'Hoffryn, who subsequently offered her the job of Vengeance Demon. Aud became Anyanka and apparently Olaf continued on his path of mayhem and destruction, eventually becoming a troll god possessed of a magic hammer. He was trapped in a crystal in the Magic Box. Anya was chattering while Willow attempted to cast a spell to create artificial sunlight and repel vampires, and she distracted Willow and sent the spell awry. (It occurs to me that we might re-attempt the spell.) The misdirected magical energy broke the crystal and released Olaf. He vandalized half of Sunnydale, the Bronze in particular, in search of ale to drink and babies to eat. His hammer is quite powerful, and after Willow sent him to the land of trolls in an alternate universe we kept his magical hammer, the weapon of a god, which was therefore capable of inflicting terrible damage.

Written after the battle with Glorificus: this god's hammer aided us in defeating her. —G

ALTERNATE UNIVERSES ARE TRICKY. SENDING SOMEONE TO A SPECIFIC UNIVERSE IS LIKE TRYING TO HIT A TARGET BY THROWING A LIVE BEE AT IT —W

Rack

Rack was a scarred warlock who supplied the demons and magic-users of Sunnydale with magical "boosts" that fed their addiction to his wares. He invaded their psyches "to take a tour" and we now know that Amy Madison had been visiting him for some time before she introduced Willow to him. He quickly singled out Willow as a "favorite" because of the great power she possessed. He told her she smelled of strawberries and indeed "Strawberry" was his nickname for her. His lair was cloaked and he moved it constantly so that only those who had the ability to find it could seek him out. After Willow renounced magics she stayed well away . . . until that terrible day when she became Dark Willow. Warren paid Rack to infuse a robot likeness with enough life force to use as a decoy so he could escape Willow. Once Willow realized what Rack had done, she drained him of all his magical essence—killing him in the process, one supposes.

FEELING VERY SORRY —W

Sid the Demon Hunter

Sid was a demon hunter who was forced by a demon's curse to dwell inside a ventriloquist puppet owned by Morgan Shay, a Sunnydale High School student. Sid had been systematically eliminating the Brotherhood of Seven, a group of demons that required human hearts and brains to retain human form. At first we assumed Morgan was the one who had killed Emily, a dancer in the talent show, and cut out her heart. Then we believed Sid was performing rituals in order to become human. I researched organ harvesting and Willow looked into reanimation theory and toys and magic. After Sid attacked Buffy, he explained about the curse and shared that, before he had been changed into a dummy, he had enjoyed "good times" with a Korean Slayer in the 1930s. When Marc the Magician was revealed to be the demon from the Brotherhood of Seven, we decapitated him with his trick guillotine and Sid stabbed him through the heart. Sid died then, free at last to move on, and we mourned the passing of a warrior.

I held Morgan's brain! I am still washing my hands! —B

And may I say, yuck! —B

I would love to know the story of how Morgan and Sid teamed up. I fear that story has been buried in the Hellmouth. —G

Troubled Teens

One cannot live one's entire life on a Hellmouth without being affected by it, I suppose. Many of Buffy's schoolmates far exceeded the dictionary definition of "troubled." I present here:

Andrew Hoelich

A member of the Sunnydale High gymnastics team who became a vampire after Buffy ran away to Los Angeles. Xander, Willow, and Oz were trying to take over her slaying duties, but Andrew was extraordinarily agile and escaped from them the night he rose. By enlisting Cordelia to act as bait, they lured him back into the cemetery, and she pushed him onto a stake held by Xander.

Precision slaying! —X

Daryl Epps

A football hero who was killed during a hiking accident. His brother Chris brought him back to life as a Frankenstein-like monster who wanted a girlfriend. Chris and his lab partner Eric Gittleson attempted to oblige Darryl by collecting fresh bits of three dead girls who had died in a car accident. But they needed fresh brain tissue: Cordelia was to provide the head.

NOT TO BE MEAN, BUT BRAIN TISSUE FROM CORDELIA? —W

Fish Boys/Gill Monsters

Dodd McAlvy, Shane West, Cameron Walker, and Gage Petronzi were among the unfortunate members of the swim team who inhaled Coach Carl Marin's brew of steroids. The potion increased their race times, but it eventually changed them into hideous green fish monsters.

AND JONATHAN CONFESSED TO PEEING IN THE POOL! ICK!
ON THE OTHER HAND . . . XANDER IN A SPEEDO! —W

They looked like the creatures from the Black Lagoon! —B

☺

I didn't know you noticed! —X

Jack O'Toole

School bully and revenant who raised his friends from the dead. He tormented Xander in life and death, and nearly blew up the school.

James Stanley

A student from the 1950s who had an affair with Grace Newman, a teacher. He shot her and then killed himself, and their ghosts haunted the school.

*Angelus and I got
possessed by them.
—B*

Justin and Zack

The boys Dawn and her friend Janice Penshaw snuck out to see on Halloween. Justin was Dawn's first kiss, but both boys turned out to be vampires. Dawn very maturely staked him whilst I effected Zack's dusting.

Do you mean you killed him?
—B

Marcie Ross

A girl so ignored by the other students that she became invisible. She wreaked revenge on many of her tormentors, but Buffy stopped her from carving up Cordelia's face. She was taken away by government agents as a promising undercover prospect.

The Pack

Kyle DuFours, Tor Hauer, Heidi Barrie, Rhonda Kelly—and Xander—became possessed by primal hyena spirits. Dr. Weirick, the zookeeper and a Primal worshipper, attempted to sacrifice Willow in order to become possessed himself, but he died instead.

Pete Clarner

Debbie Foley's abusive boyfriend created a Dr. Jekyll-and-Mr. Hyde-type elixir that supercharged his violent, brutal nature. He ended by killing her.

Sheila Martini

A violent delinquent in competition with Buffy who would likely get the Slayer expelled if Parent-Teacher Night was not a success. Spike abducted her as a meal for Drusilla. She was transformed into a vampire and was a member of Spike's raiding party at the school. She attempted to do Buffy in with an axe but ran off.

I heard she slaughtered everyone at The Fish Tank, that bar she likes to go to.
—B

Tucker Wells

The older brother to Andrew Wells of the Geek Trio; he trained hellhounds to attack the prom.

GRRRR!
FORMAL WEAR!
—W

The Ugly Man

Young Billy Palmer lay in a coma in Sunnydale Hospital after being beaten senseless. He projected his fear of "the Ugly Man"—his attacker—as a violent bald monster with a bulbous, mottled face and one milky eye. Whilst Billy's projection of himself roamed the halls of the school, our own worst nightmares came true as well: failing tests, appearing naked, spiders. Xander was pursued by a horrifying clown; Willow had to perform an opera; Cordelia was an unfashionable member of the chess club. Buffy believed her father hated her and that she had been turned into a vampire, that the Master lived. And for me … Buffy lay dead beneath her headstone as a result of my ineptitude as Watcher. The Ugly Man attacked a Sunnydale High School student named Laura, who was able to tell us that he said "lucky nineteen." Buffy put two and two together and realized that was Billy's Kiddie League player number. Billy unmasked the Ugly Man of his astral-projection dream and the demonic creature vanished. When his coach walked into his hospital room, the "real" Billy awoke and confirmed that the coach himself had beaten Billy because he blamed the boy for losing the game.

That's putting it mildly! —B

Actually Giles, that would be "one" and "nine." —B

Werewolves

To my way of thinking, werewolves are humans who transform into wolf-beings for three nights—before and after the full moon, and during the full moon itself. They become ravening beasts—large four-legged wolflike creatures with pointed ears, extended muzzles, fearsome teeth, and sharp claws. They are aggressive predators and thus are rightly locked up at sunset for those three nights. But they are still human.

When I first met Daniel Osbourne (Oz), he was the taciturn lead guitarist for Dingoes Ate My Baby, a popular local band. His young cousin Jordy turned him into a werewolf after a playful bite. Oz hid this condition from us, and feared that he had killed his bandmate Jeffrey Walken (we later discovered that the perpetrator was Pete Clarner). He was pursued by the werewolf hunter Gib Cain, who took the opposite viewpoint from mine: that werewolves were inhuman monsters who looked and acted like humans, much like vampires when they are not feeding. He bragged to us that he had killed eleven werewolves.

Veruca was also a musician, the lead singer for a band called Shy. She was much more comfortable in her werewolf skin, freely hunting and thinking nothing

Cain was a total pig. I'm glad I bent his gun. I should have bent something else. —B

of mating with Oz while they were both transformed. Willow and the rest of us saw this quite differently, of course. Veruca savagely stalked and attacked Willow, leaving Oz no choice but to kill Veruca.

Overwhelmed, he left Sunnydale to seek a cure and returned triumphant many months later: in Tibet, he had learned to tame his inner savage beast with meditation, herbs, and charms. However, he soon realized that he now had a rival for Willow's affections: Tara Maclay. So great was his jealousy that he transformed into a werewolf in full daylight—which I had never heard of—and attacked Tara. The Initiative captured him and tortured him "for research purposes," forcing him to change through extreme pain. Once freed, he bade us farewell and <u>we've not seen him since.</u>

MAYBE SOMEDAY HE'LL
COME BACK? —W

Other Forces of Darkness

Conclusion

Apocalypses
& Magic Spells

The Master Attempts To Open The Hellmouth

MAGICS USED: *"For they will gather and be gathered, from the Vessel pours life and out of the crescent moon, the first past the solstice it will come."*
The Master anointed Luke to drain teenagers to give him the power to escape.

HOW WE STOPPED HIM: HE GOT OUT, BUT BUFFY STAKED HIM

The Demon Acathla Nearly Sucks The World Into Hell

MAGICS USED: Angelus fed Acathla his own blood and pulled out a binding sword to start the ritual. *"Everything that I am, everything that I have done, has led me here."*

HOW WE STOPPED HIM: UM, WELL . . .   *It's all right, Will. We need to write it down. I stabbed Angel and sent him to hell. —B*

Vahrall Demons Perform The Sacrifice Of Three

MAGICS USED: The three demons jumped into the Hellmouth with the blood of a male human, the bones of a child, and the Word of Valios, a talisman.

HOW WE STOPPED THEM: BUFFY PULLED ONE OF THE DEMONS OUT OF THE HELLMOUTH AND IT DIED. THE RITUAL FAILED.

DEMONS OF THE HELLMOUTH

THERE WERE ACTUALLY THIRTEEN MAJOR APOCALYPSES
BEFORE WE GOT THE OL' HELLMOUTH CLOSED BUT
THESE ARE THE TOP SIX (WE TOOK A VOTE!).
—W

Glorificus Opens The Portal To Her Own Hell Dimension

MAGICS USED: *"The blood flows, the gates will open; the gates will close when it flows no more."* Glory's worshipper Doc spilled Dawn's blood.

HOW WE STOPPED HER: GILES SMOTHERED BEN; BEN DIED, AND GLORY DIED WITH HIM. BUFFY
DOVE INTO THE MYSTICAL ENERGY OF THE GATE AND SAVED DAWN. ☹

But it's okay
Will! I'm here!
—B

Dark Willow Tries To Drain The Earth's Life Energy Through An Effigy Of Proserpexa

MAGICS USED: *"From the pit of forgotten shadows . . . Awaken, sister of the dark, awaken . . . Proserpexa . . . Let the cleansing fires from the depths burn away the suffering souls . . . And bring sweet death."* Then Willow conjured earth monsters of dirt with fibrous root-claws to slow Buffy down.

HOW WE STOPPED ME: XANDER GOT THROUGH TO THE "GOOD" ME,
AND I STOPPED. I'M SO SORRY. ☹

Final Battle At The Hellmouth Against The First Evil

MAGICS USED : The First Evil used Caleb, Bringers, and sympathetic demons to open the Seal of Danzalthar and send a horde of thousands of Turok-Han to enter our world. Willow prepared herself to go beyond the darkest place she'd ever been.

HOW WE STOPPED IT:

I ENCHANTED THE SCYTHE SO THAT ALL THE POTENTIALS BECAME SLAYERS.
SPIKE WORE AN ENCHANTED AMULET THAT DREW DOWN THE POWER OF THE SUN.
IT BURNED ALL THE TUROK-HAN . . . AND SPIKE TOO.

AND WE WON!

DEMONS OF THE HELLMOUTH

My Final Thoughts

As I look over this Guide, I feel quite astonished that I am still *here*. I must confess as well to a bit of <u>atavistic</u> Watcher pride that my Slayer survived all this *and* the Battle of the Hellmouth, too. And that she *also* changed the destiny of all Slayers everywhere, giving them lives undreamed of by Slayers past. And so in that spirit, I have asked Buffy herself to add a few lines to this guide to the Demons of the Hellmouth before we continue <u>the quest that is our duty: to fight evil where we find it.</u>

Giles, dictionary? —B

For some really good new shoes Perhaps with heels. —B

Dear Slayers,

When I asked Willow to use her magical powers to change you from Potentials to Slayers, I also asked you if agreed to what that meant. You said yes.

Some of us died in the final battle, and the world might never know about the ultimate price we paid.

But you know, and I know. We closed the Hellmouth and stopped The First. But the fight isn't over for us, and it never will be. Into this generation, we

Slayers have been born. I asked you once, and I ask you again: Are you ready to be strong?

With love,
Buffy the Vampire Slayer

Demons of the Hellmouth: A Guide for Slayers
ISBN 978-1-783293384

Published by Titan Books
A division of Titan Publishing Group Ltd.
144 Southwark St.
London
SE1 0UP

First edition: September 2015
24681097531

Demons of the Hellmouth: A Guide for Slayers
is produced by becker&mayer! Book Producers, Bellevue, Washington.
www.beckermayer.com
13267

Author: Nancy Holder
Designer: Rosebud Eustace
Editors: Kjersti Egerdahl, Dana Youlin, and Ruth Austin
Image Researchers: Emily Zach and Donna Metcalf
Production Coordinator: Tom Miller

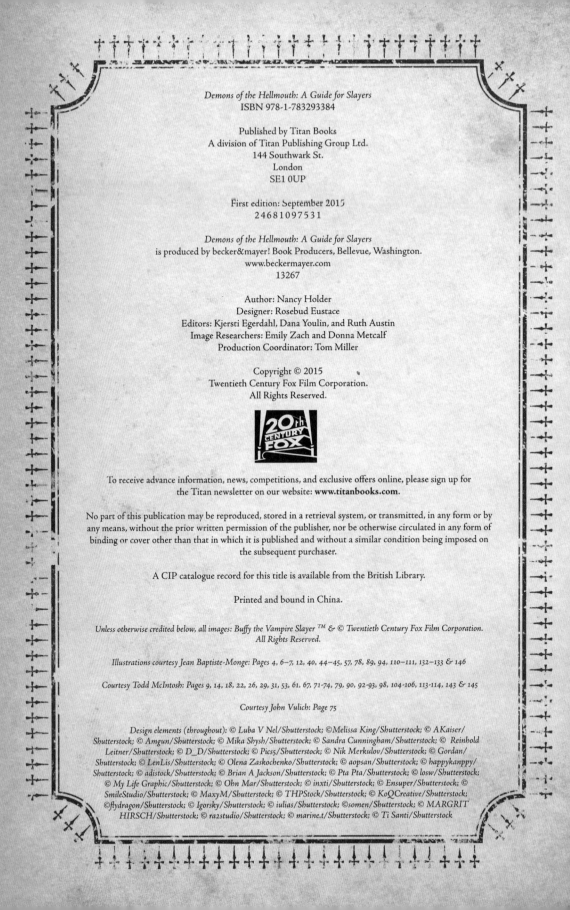

To receive advance information, news, competitions, and exclusive offers online, please sign up for
the Titan newsletter on our website: **www.titanbooks.com**.

A CIP catalogue record for this title is available from the British Library.

Printed and bound in China.